The Stafford Challenge 2024-25 Anthology

Edited by Brian Rohr

WILD POET PRESS • BEAVERTON, OREGON

Anthology Copyright © 2025 by Wild Poet Press
All poems used with permission by the authors.
Copyrights to individual poems belong to the authors.

All rights reserved. No part of this publication may be reproduced, distributed, or transmitted in any form by any means, including photocopying, recording, or other electronic methods, nor used for the purposes of training AI, without the prior written permission of the author, except in the case of brief quotations embodied in reviews and certain other noncommercial uses permitted by copyright law. For permission requests, write to the author at the email address below.

Published by:
Wild Poet Press
Beaverton, Oregon
news@staffordchallenge.com

Cover design: Brian Rohr
Layout design: Tod McCoy

Library of Congress Control Number: 2025906219
Print ISBN: 979-8-9985119-0-5
Ebook ISBN: 979-8-9985119-1-2

First edition.

This book is dedicated to those who have joined The Stafford Challenge community and to anyone who has ever felt the deep pull of language, creativity, and the desire to express something potent and true.

It is also dedicated to the memory of William Stafford. May there always be another generation of inspired readers for his poetry.

Deep gratitude to Regina Beach, Tod McCoy, and Jennifer White for their incredible help with this anthology. Their support and expertise have made this book possible.

Table of Contents

Brian Rohr • Introduction	xi
Mary Anne Abdo • Effervescent Soul	1
Amber Albritton • Coming or Leaving	2
Stacy Allen, Lesley Barker, Jessi Kim, and Pamir Kiciman • After Jackals	4
Linda Knowlton Appel • The Breath of Gaia	5
Ann Arbor • Where We're Going	6
Samantha Arthurs • Heart & Soul	7
Kate Ballew • Legacy	8
Leita Barlow • With You, Alone	9
Tyler Barrett • Aqueous Solution	10
Gretchen Bartels-Ray • Connie	11
Regina Beach • The Firehose of Life	12
Christine Beauchaine • The Clock Is Gone	14
Sarah Beckett • Dry Your Tears	15
Anita Bondi • Quilting in Sixty Seconds	16
Karen Bonnell • Caring for Our Children	17
Patricia Brenneman • Lazarus	18
Deb Brod • To My Mother, Again	19
Susan Brown • Tabernacle	21
Jennifer Browne • In a Period of Absence, She Remembers a Dream	23
Rebecca Burgener • Soar and Pour	26
Sarah Diamond Burroway • Uninvited Guests on a February Morning	28
Kendall S. Cable • Wolf Full Moon	29
Jillian Calahan • Forbidden	30
Sam Calhoun • Winter Solstice 2024	31
Necia Campbell • Lyric Handshake, a Friendship Ghazal	32
Nancy Capranica Carlson • On Becoming God	33
Diane Carmony • The Office of Dr. W.D. Hutchings (Madison, Indiana)	35
C.A. Carpenter • The Last Day	36
Mary Carter • How to Exhume an Old Woman from 1450	37
Jenn Cavanaugh • Futility	39
Dela Coleman-Posey • Quiet	40

Tim Conroy • Bloodstone	41
Margaret Coombs • February Program on the Birds of Costa Rica	42
Susan Michele Coronel • Wish	43
Lisa Cottrell • What Age Did You Realize Death?	44
Cathren Cougill • Sorry It's Been a While	46
Glenda Cowen-Funk • Fault Lines	48
Barbara Crary • Play/Ground	49
Colette Crown • Humans Can Be Museums	50
Karla Daniel • Courage	51
Laura Daniels • Dagger	52
Jeanice Eagan Davis • I Have Wasted My Life	53
Lee Desrosiers • Uses for a Stick	54
Tamera Neilson Dobbins • Health and Time Are Life's Treasure	55
Branwen Drew • The New Year	56
Barbara Edler • Snow	57
Whisper Edwards • An Ache that Never Thaws	58
Aaliyah El-Amin • A Plate of Grief	59
Leslie Enzian • The Privacy of Them	60
Karin Evans • Dark Waters	62
R.G. Evans • Grace Notes	63
Helena Fagan • Disquiet	64
Anna Finch • Our Voices	65
Mary Eichhorn Fletcher • Beaver Moon, Midnight	66
Judith-Kate Friedman • Beyond the Ballet	67
Tammy Forner • Climate Change	68
CMarie Fuhrman • Between Desire and Expectation	70
Kathleen Fullerton • The Space Between	71
Trina Gaynon • Pharaohs, Carpenters, and Leafcutters	72
Cathy George • We the People	73
Fred Gerhard • The End of a Sonnet Is Not the End of the Poem	74
Tanya Gogo • Rising	75
Renata Golden • Jane	76
Becky Goodwin • Oh Possibility!	77
Ali Grimshaw • Belief in Planting	78
Susan Haifleigh • Waiting for Grace	79
Emilia Haley • Sounds Depicted from a Monday Afternoon	80
Jonathan Hall • Perspective	81
Katherine Hancock • Winter	82

MJ Hatfield • Petrichor	83
Christine Havens • Short Serenade for Putty and Strings	84
Melissa Helton • (Re)Forest	85
Haley Hnatuk • A Haunting	86
Bob Hoeppner • Wake	87
Jonathan Horwitz • The Choice	88
Robert Hughes • Jean Vigo	89
Marie Linde Husby • Writer's Block	90
Shelli Hutchinson • In the Beginning	91
Mary Imo-Stike • Be Here with Me	92
Cynthia Jacobi • Orderliness	93
Holly Jahangiri • Throwaway Planet	94
Nancy Jentsch • Snow and Soil	95
Kim Johnson • Mornings in Eden	96
Marilyn Johnston • Dear Mr. Stafford	98
Libby Falk Jones • Alone, Together	99
Lisa Kagan • Alphabet of the Moment	101
Gayle Kaune • At the Zoo	102
Sarah Keeney • Hobbies	103
Ellen Girardeau Kempler • On the Day of Donald J. Trump's Election as 47th President of the United States: Notice What This Poem Is Not Doing	104
Pamela Kenley-Meschino • Narrative Assignment	105
Liz Kingsley • A Haiku	106
Sabrina Kirby • January 9, 2025	107
Cynthia Briggs Kittredge • Frostbit Bamboo	108
Denise Krebs • Remember	109
Michael Lainoff • Ode to an Albatross	110
Martha Landman • Like Mistletoe	111
Christina Valentine Larsen • Adulting	113
M.E. Lee • Confidence	114
Cathy Cultice Lentes • Limen	115
Deanna Lernihan • Untitled, in the Garden	116
Kath Lieffort • Antiques Roadshow	118
Anna Christine Linder-Skach • Anna Christine Imagines Her Funeral	119
Susan J. Littlefield • Re-Claiming Warrior Within	121
Svetlana Litvinchuk • Alive Forever	122
Kristinoel Ludwig • Morning Haiku	123
Emilie Lygren • Love Letter to the Moon	124

M. L. Lyons • Embrace Me, Earthling	125
Dory Maguire • Genealogy	126
Stacie Marinelli • Foxtrot	127
Dorothy P. Marshall • Untethered	128
Catherine Lynn Martell • I Am One	129
Karen McCaskey • Awakening	130
Jay McCoy • Aftercare	131
Tod McCoy • Wellness Check	132
Megan McDonald • Listen to Poets	133
Wendy McVicker • Half a Poem	134
Paige Mengel • Letting Go	135
Abby Meysenburg • The Robin and the Worm	136
Kimberly A. Miller • Miracle in a Cup	137
Paula Baughman Miller • Night Warrior	138
Clayton Moon • Amber Ember	139
Misha Moon • Let Me Love This Horrible World	142
Kate McCarroll Moore • Ode to My Old Hands	143
Chandra Tyler Mountain • You'll Hear Music	144
Charly Mullan • 25 Stars!	145
NanLeah • Summer Stars	146
Bonnie Naradzay • Cloud of Unknowing	147
Joseph Neely • Forsythe Junior High	148
Will Nixon • Everything	149
Naomi Shihab Nye • Marfa	150
Jenny Olson • Silhouettes at Night	151
Carol Clemente O'Malley • Reflections	153
Heather Oneal • Finding Beauty	154
Diane O'Neill • What Is the Meaning?	155
Kate O'Neill • Before You Leave Joyce Country	156
Asher Packman • The Forge of Being	157
Donna M. Padgett • "Will She Get Over It?" "She Will Never Get Over It!"	158
Steve Paul • The Columbines Grow	159
Jane Pearson • So Much Killing	160
Sarah Josephine Pennington • (An American Sentence, In a Private Room on the Med Surg Floor, 2021)	161
Charles A. Perrone • Overture to a Dramatic Monologue	162
Shannon Perry • Kinship of Douglas Firs	163
Crissy Anderson Peters • A Prayer for Lent	165
Mary Louise Peters • Some Questions	166
Jennifer Pratt-Walter • Antlers	167

Vanessa Proctor • Library	168
Quigley Provost-Landrum • On Seeing Krapp's Last Tape	169
Melissa Rankin • Meditation Run	170
Cindy Redman • Like Water	171
Amy Le Ann Richardson • We're All Pulled	172
Cathy Rigg • Winter Laid Wide	173
Kaci Rigney • Full Cart	174
Richard Robbins • The Wake	175
Sheila DC Robertson • Blankets of Cold	176
Zoé Y. Robles • Flamma Vestalis	177
Adriana Rocha • Bird of Words	178
Joe Roche • The Sweet, Sweet Spot	179
Tamarah Rockwood • Metamorphosis	180
Shelly Rodrigue • Wheelbarrow	181
Brian Rohr • Once, a Crow Broke Free	182
Jennifer Rood • Love Letter	183
Michael Running • Rocks of Solitude	184
June Crawford Sanders • Mom's Word Salad	185
Leslayann Schecterson • Red Dirt Ditty	186
Lisa Shahon • Thursday Morning, 7:20am	187
Ron Shapiro • Ode to Tofu	188
Erin T. Sim • Promises	190
Margaret Simon • Live Oak Pantoum	191
Andy Smith • Small Wall	192
Gerard Donnelly Smith • The Real Estate Sale	193
Nora Snyder • A Christmas Plan That Became a Christmas Unplanned... and Led by the Itching of My Fingertips	195
Liane Sousa • Silence	196
Kim Stafford • Bagel Boy	197
Kristina Stapleton • Escape of the MS Rotterdam	198
John Stickney • Future Visit	199
D. Yohanna Storm • My High Priestess of Prayer	200
Mark Strohschein • Let Me Begin Again	203
Jessica Swafford • To Tell the Cats	204
David M. Sweet • Turning a Corner	205
Connie Taylor • A Duck's Back	206
Jo Taylor • Tacos, Cracks and Song	207
Dawn Thompson • Thaw	208
David Traylor • New Flyer	209
Kathryn True • The Balance of Things	211

Gail Hathaway Tupper • Untitled	212
Lesley Tyson • The Dream Was a Lie	213
Mary Vee • Ice	214
Jayne R. Vondrak • In the Honeycomb of My Bones	215
Lynn J. Walters • Blessings and Love	216
Cathy Warner • Morning Prayer	217
Seth Warren • Island of the Narrow	218
Crystal L. White • What Dream Touches	219
Jennifer R. White • The Gift of Ages	220
Brenda Wildrick • Flames Rapidly Spreading	221
Dana Wildsmith • Everything Else Falls Away	223
Tim Wiles • Safe at Home	224
Jake Williams • To an Easter Craiglockhart Elm	225
Steve Williams • Proper Space and Shape?	226
Jessica Wolf • I Know Love	227
Beth Wolfe • I'm Not Here to Smile Because it Makes You Happy	228
Gloria Wu • Inextinguishable	229
Diosa Xochiquetzalcóatl • At a Library Somewhere in SoCal	231
Anya Zamiar • Street Crossing	232
Norma Zimmermann • Ship Wrecked	233
Poetry Unlocked My Cell: Our Stafford Challenge Parting Poem	234

BRIAN ROHR
FOUNDER AND DIRECTOR OF THE STAFFORD CHALLENGE

Introduction

There is an old idea that spoken and written words carry magic, that they hold power in themselves while also shaping meaning in our wild and unpredictable world. As a poet, I take this to heart. The words we choose, when woven into a poem, have the ability to invite, awaken, heal, or even to wound and harm. Words are not neutral, they carry meaning, energy, and the power to transform.

It is this belief in the power and delight of words that led me to create The Stafford Challenge.

The poems in this collection represent a fraction of the many thousands of poems written between January 17, 2024, and January 16, 2025 by The Stafford Challenge 2024 cohort. Each poem in this collection is a tribute to the commitment and creative drive of these remarkable poets, written within the structure of this challenge.

What Is The Stafford Challenge?
In the fall of 2023, an idea arrived during a long, hot shower. As a poet and storyteller, I was searching for a way to deepen my writing practice. As a father working full-time, I found that my creative output wasn't what I wished it to be. I knew I wrote more when I had structure, a container for my creativity. Recalling the impressive and prolific daily writing practice of the late, great poet William Stafford, I committed to writing a poem every day for a year. I was excited and inspired. But as I considered embarking on this challenge, I realized I didn't want to do it alone.

Who would I invite? Who else might want to join in? I could ask a few poet friends, of course, but what if I opened the door wider? What if anyone who wanted to join could do so?

I reached out to Kim Stafford, a poet and writer of great renown in his own right, and the son of William Stafford. As the executor of his father's literary estate, Kim graciously gave his blessing to use his father's name and likeness for the project. With that blessing, The Stafford Challenge was born, and to my astonishment, it took off like wildfire.

Not knowing whether 50 or 100 people might sign up that first year, I was floored when 1,153 people from 28 countries and 49 U.S. states (plus Washington, D.C.) joined in. What came forth was more than just a writing challenge; it became a vibrant, generous, and deeply supportive creative community.

The Stafford Challenge 2024 Community
As a way to celebrate our coming together and to provide a central meeting place, we created a private Facebook group open only to those who signed up for The Challenge. Nearly 600 participants chose to join the group. At first it was a beautiful sea of creative chaos, overwhelming our feeds with introductions and poems. It was glorious and made it much more fun to be on the platform. With a few rules and guidelines to keep the posts poetry-focused, it quickly became our community center, our coffee house, our town square, our gathering place. We settled into a rhythm of poems and questions shared and responses and reactions given. We had a rule that no critiques could be given unless someone specifically asked for them. Many did ask, and used the feedback as a way to workshop and improve their poems. Others used the group as a way to stay accountable, posting daily to ensure they stayed on top of their poem-a-day commitment.

During a difficult year, with global wars and a divisive electoral season, the group became a balm of kindness and support: A reminder that the power of humanity and creativity can thrive.

The Stafford Challenge Guest Poets
One of the highlights of The Stafford Challenge was the monthly Guest Poet presentations. These presentations offered an opportunity for us to learn and be moved by some of the finest poets writing today. These sessions offered moments of depth, reflection, inspiration, and connection as fuel to support us in our year-long commitment.

Starting with Kim Stafford, our inaugural Guest Poet, he set the tone for the year with warmth, humor, and wisdom, suggesting that poetry can be used as a practice about paying attention to ourselves and the world around us. He spoke about his father's writing practice, offering insight, and a format, into the daily discipline that inspired The Stafford Challenge.

Mona Lisa Saloy, Ph.D., past Poet Laureate of Louisiana, brought a vibrant energy, weaving history, storytelling, and rhythm into her talk while Emmett Wheatfall charged us, saying poets were modern day prophets.

Naomi Shihab Nye left us spellbound, speaking of poetry as a vehicle for peace and understanding in hard times. Each Guest Poet brought something unique, offering us new ways to think about poetry, creativity, and the art of writing. These sessions became grounding points throughout the year, giving us moments to pause, reflect, and recharge.

The full list of 2024 Guest Poets includes: Kim Stafford*, Mona Lisa Saloy, Ph.D.*, Emmett Wheatfall, Georgia Popoff*, Lauren Camp*, Jessica Jacobs, Emilie Lygren, Marcela Sulak, Naomi Shihab Nye, CMarie Fuhrman*, John Rosenwald, and Pádraig Ó Tuama. (*Current or past poet laureates.)

Honoring the Poets of The Stafford Challenge
Writers of all backgrounds from seasoned poets to first-time writers showed up for themselves and each other during The Stafford Challenge. They proved that poetry and community thrives when given space to grow, and that when we commit ourselves to a daily creative act, we awaken something powerful and important within.

This collection is a celebration of the work produced by this remarkable community, a small sampling of the vast and varied poetry that has been written, shared, and cherished over the past year. It is a reminder that words matter, that stories and poems shape us, and that when we gather around the fire of creativity, something sacred and enduring is kindled.

May your words be blessed with magic and power, and may they be a force of good in a difficult world. And when doubt, hardship, or even joy threaten to silence you, remember this: When the world surprises you, don't stop writing.

Learn more about The Stafford Challenge at staffordchallenge.com.

BRIAN ROHR

When the World Surprises You, Don't Stop Writing

When the world surprises you, don't stop writing,
even if the systems you know break.

War may shatter, plans may be dashed,
dreams may come true,
whatever you do, do not stop writing.

Do not stop writing when they say, I love you, but…
Do not stop writing when they say, I love you, and…
Do not stop when they say, your performance could have been…
or was worthy of…

Keep going when you get the call you've longed for,
or dreaded to receive.

Keep on, keep on.
Don't stop when your unpaid bill arrives with a letter.
Don't stop when you are on the ground, bloodied, broken,
unused or used up.

When a storm or fire comes, and you are tired,
and going on means going on and on,
don't stop writing.

When your teacher dies,
or your friend dies,
and more people you know keep dying,
don't stop writing.

When life is in your womb
and you don't know to celebrate or cry,
write. Write.

When the kids are scared, and you are scared
and the walls around you crumble,
tend as you need to tend,
but don't stop writing.

Keep on.

When all the books have been read
all the years, lived
all the tears, shed

when all the words have been spoken
all the grime cleansed,
the dust settled,

even then,
even then,
don't stop writing.

When the light dims,
the echo fades,
the last thought breathes,
and you remember a life,

don't stop, until you truly know,
that it is the end.

Then, let go,
and fade into the sweet night's wind.

MARY ANNE ABDO
Effervescent Soul

Our souls are never inside,
of our bodies' encasement.
Our souls are living and breathing.
Circling outside of our bodies.
An encapsulation of light.
Enabling us to share that light,
with others.
Uplifting light.
Loving light.
Compassionate light.
Joyful light.
Playful light.
Warm light.
It is a radiant light.
It is a totality of light
Our own personal sunlight.

AMBER ALBRITTON
Coming or Leaving

If you're ready to go, go.
I'll always be thankful for you.
We've both tried to leave
In our own ways, twice before.
I don't want you to go but if I'm asked
To accept it, I guess I'll have to.
What I want is for you to come watch
This movie with me, *Gladiator II*,
Of poetry & warrior, Michael,
One cannot seem to escape the other,
And it's of love & parental sacrifice.
Both, we know all too well.
You specifically, I want to run my curiosities
Past, my day to days, & those bigger thoughts
That others don't have the faculty of imagination
To touch. I want your friendship. I want you
To mentor me through this transition of ethics,
Of nonmonogamy, & it's true, we're in two different
Relationships, to & with one another. Everyone is.

I had a date this morning, another apricot pucker
This evening. Including all I don't remember
Monday, that will be six. Dates, all lesser than
The one I call lover in the waking hours & in the dark
Hours between dusk & dawn, & when I dream, it's you.
And that's the one you're really worried about.
I would like to know you; not continuing
to know you is an aggravation, a dropped twenty
A breathless pain, & an irritant of ache in my eyes.
But I'm nothing to you any longer, not nothing but
Not a tree, nor a bench, nor a slap, nor a slab of slate
by the blue heron, nor a cup of coffee. I'm not
A concert. I'm not a movie. I'm not an overnight stay.
I'm not banana bread, not a snowball fight,
Or giant snow angels or sledding, not cold hands blown
Into, your breath & gargantuan mits warming mine.

I'm not a shared song, picture, meme, or poem. Not
Even a lousy lay. I am a broken mood & a wasted
Month of Mondays.

STACY ALLEN, LESLEY BARKER, JESSI KIM, PAMIR KICIMAN
After Jackals

A collaborative poem by members of the Stafford Challenge Small Group E12

When the planets align and the stars collide,
The hands of cosmos clap
The Earth halts, threatening to teeter backward
Brooks hush their babbles, fawns lift their bobbleheads
And for the first time, I stop and open my eyes.

Eyes wide open, that's what we were told
When valleys weren't blazed and the sun wasn't burnt umber
Waters were clear and mountains hadn't collapsed
Young hearts gave the fight, but the jackals scorched it all.

They laugh, the jackals as if theirs was the last word.
As if gray ash and black cinders, flimsy though they are, marked the end of it all.
But, hear now the sound of a mighty, rushing wind
Escorting loud thunder, and torrential rain.

Lightning illuminates the antelope tribe
They run, triumphant, as new rivers form to sweep the jackals away
Storm subsides. Parched ground reveals a burst of green here, a wildflower there
New life begins, even as the stars collide.

LINDA KNOWLTON APPEL
The Breath of Gaia

The copper light of yesterday's sunset
has given way to the soft silver light of this
silent new day. And Gaia breathes.
The world contracts in a slow exhalation,
and light rises one minute later this morning
than last, and the leaves lie limp on lofty limbs,
preparing to drift gently downward
in the backglow of autumn.
I exhale and inhale slowly and deeply
to capture the spice of the elderly garden.
I scuff though piles of leaves the dogs
have disturbed; in the day's soft warmth
they crinkle loudly beneath my feet.
The gold and copper hues are Gaia's gift,
a reminder that this long contraction is
but one beat in her song of the seasons.

ANN ARBOR
Where We're Going

Outside the kitchen window
brittle leaves chase each other
like spring squirrels
over the crusty snow.

The wind intends to turn
everything topsy-turvy
depositing one frozen leaf
in every depressed deer print.
Whatever the outside
temperature may be,
it's colder than that.

Complaining may soothe
some of us, but it won't
be as useful as we hope.
It's time to put on
our "we're-really-grown-up" pants
and start walking.

Each step matters
even if we, personally,
never get where we're going.

SAMANTHA ARTHURS
Heart & Soul

My heart is an old growth forest
All hardwoods and bramble
Full of mist in the mornings
Humid and damp by afternoon

A most unusual space full of
All things both seen and unseen
A shadow at the corner of your eye
Strange voices calling your name

I am this place that made me
A daughter of mountain people and
Country churches, in both God's house
And the mysteries made by his hand

I am Appalachian
Heart and soul

KATE BALLEW
Legacy

Hands wet
From river or well
Women walking miles to gather water from Earth's estuaries
Ashen soap pulling oils from skin submerged daily
Century after century
Hands of women washing
Washing clothes
Washing food
Washing babies
Washing men's backs and crotches
Washing dishes pot and pans
Hands hardened pulling weeds and crops
Hands wrapping stems of hay and stalks of corn and wheat
Bundles and mounds in endless fields
Hands working in heat and rain and cold
Ancestors sold into servitude
Multitudes cleaning and clearing a path for me
Hands wet
In my sink filled with hot water from an electric tank
Flowing into sinks and tubs and showers
In my home
Bought and brought to me by ancestors unknown
Hands wet
Gloved by water that has fallen to earth over and over and over
Rising back into clouds and storms that I will never see

LEITA BARLOW
With You, Alone

When the silence screams so loudly
covering the ears does not help
begging for words to form
to explain the loss
the disappearance within a chasm so dark
I cannot feel you anymore
I hear your groans of age, of grief perhaps
but I do not know
for your lips are sealed, and your heart seems as well
So, I walk, quietly out
into the night
Out beyond the loneliness of being with you

TYLER BARRETT
Aqueous Solution

The water behind my eyes
building atmospheric pressure,
cutting off oxygen.
Rapidly fading and wondering
why the hell I'm even writing this.

Everything burns like frost
on idealistic summer skin.
Am I broken?
or
Maybe I've done all I was meant to do here.
Maybe all the good has bled out of me.
How do I know?
And where are the instructions
on how to dissolve,
because this highlight reel in my head is agony.

GRETCHEN BARTELS-RAY
Connie

She named the rocket Connie,

and nighttimes now
we watch the grainy cellphone video
of the distant rocket
and its glowing contrail.

I bask in the stereo chorus
of her laughter—recorded and live—
Connie, Connie, Connie, she calls,
believing the whole universe can hear her

and will reply in friendship.

REGINA BEACH

The Firehose of Life

I made my own life hard in the before times
Before it was made harder by lack of mobility
A peg leg and an inner ear that doesn't know which way's up

I made my own life hard by caring too much
Taking on the world
Being bothered by little things
Drinking from the firehose of life
Walking around wet and disheveled
Thinking that one day my lips might fit around the giant nozzle
And that I'd become omniscient
Doing it all, having it all, severed into a thousand versions of myself
Transporting the multiverse into this one short life
Attempting everything ensures nothing gets done

I used to wring the resilience from my students' sleeves
Like it was a foregone conclusion that the least-resourced amongst us
Should automatically be able to dig deep
And find the extra capacity to thrive
At the end of the stick
In the midst of distraction
The drama of hunger, violence, cold, chaos,
the unpredictability of a life without a safety net

And now I find myself in a precarious place
Told I'm resilient, that I'm inspirational
For simply rising from bed and getting "out there"
As if the expectations were still that the disabled
Should be neither seen nor heard
That it would be reasonable for me to simply
Wither away at home where no one can observe
My stilted walking, my erratic bladder,
Where I can furniture surf my way to the
Amazon delivery rather
Than trundle out to the shops

Resilient is not what you're born with
It's what they call you when you've lived through
Something they wouldn't want to endure
When you've come out the other end better than expected
Defying logic or stereotype

Resilience is to exist on the margins of a world that prizes nothing
More than perfect, healthy bodies
Young ones, beautiful ones
Ones without trauma or history or tragedy

CHRISTINE BEAUCHAINE
The Clock Is Gone

The clock is gone
I dreamed about a grandfather clock last night
We had one once
A small version
That your grandparents gave us as a wedding present
In another lifetime
It stopped working at some point
And it didn't make it through the last move
Or maybe the one before that
So many things just stopped working
And couldn't be carried forward
Into this new life
The clock is gone

SARAH BECKETT
Dry Your Tears

Yes, I know
the news is bad—but look
there is beauty in this world,
where clouds lark about in their fields of blue
chasing each other across the sky;
where a man and a woman entwine their arms
and walk along the water's edge,
burnished black-gold in the morning sun.

Dry your tears,
there is beauty here
in the language of the unsaid,
where the flame-trees flower
and pelicans still cross the bay at dusk,
unafraid of the approaching night
host to a thousand astonished stars
and the sea, rocked in the moon's forgiving light.

ANITA BONDI
Quilting in Sixty Seconds

Let's come together and stitch this
Thing called home
Gather each square
Unmatching
All glorious colors
Patterns shapes
A rainbow
Of life living
Pain, joy the whole
Enchilada
Or simply, humanness.
Let's come together and stir
The pot of a thousand
Ingredients that just might
Blend
Well
If given the chance.
This task is ours
All of us
Brass and wood
Tile and stone
Lie down together
Find each puzzle piece
Align sky and grass
Maybe even catch a falling star
Figure out the beauty
And the difference
It makes
If you let your lips turn
Into
Smile.

KAREN BONNELL
Caring for Our Children

Her wrestle is deep. She is fully four years
with all the uncertainty around the edges
that comes with being born.
Her watery imagination full of sharks and clown fish…

I watch her lost in an inner world, talking to unseen friends,
naming invented games, sharing willingly, reciprocity accepted
practicing how to be in her world
practicing and practicing.

She dips out for a moment to ask permission,
"Can I bring out the bubble wands and pretend with them?"
"Of course," and back she goes.
I was so like her—more content in that world than any other.

The real world can be chafing, a biting winter wind—
leaving exposed little beings, their tender nerve endings
rough and reddened, begging for a gentle tone
for warm hands slathered with lotion

ready to sooth and protect.

PATRICIA BRENNEMAN
Lazarus

Lying there in corpse pose,
his favorite asana—
the release of it, the relief of it
after all those warrior poses
and core work,
the wrapping of muscles around bones,
lifting here, dropping there.
Ah, here, bundled, he thinks
—blankets around me all tucked in,
weighted lavender pillow on my eyes—
I just want to rest here for a good while.
The voice when it comes is abrupt,
insistent.
No soft gentle guidance to wriggle
      his toes and fingers, to make delicate
      micro movements, to stretch, to
      rock the head slowly back and forth.
No invitation to roll onto one side or
      another, to rest there for a moment
      before—slowly—propping himself up.
None of these.
Instead: Arise!
And it's done. He's on his feet, dizzy,
      disoriented, the wrappings that
      held him, on the ground at his feet.
The light too bright.
Everyone's joy, too much.
I just wanted to rest, he says.

DEB BROD
To My Mother, Again

your little orchids
they're with me now, hanging on,
whispering your name

wondering where you
are, when you left, when you will
touch their leaves with yours

your gentle fingers,
delicate petals floating
too long in water

losing mastery
over your lush world of touch,
making, acquiring

and massaging my
floppy little ego, soft
as dying orchid

petals, without a
prayer, hopeful anyway,
even when your mind

catches fire and your
flames devour me, head to toe,
burning the roots that

earthed me, the seed that
birthed me. merciless. where are
you? not to drag you

through the mud again,
but where are your fingers, so
soft, transparently

ready for the world
once, poised, in tune, opening
only opening?

SUSAN BROWN
Tabernacle

Prelude: Hiram washed the diesel odor off
along with the grime of their coal run job
changed to shirt and silk tie
hopped off train 962, walked two blocks south
he was due to preach at 7 sharp

Some sinners felt guilt entering the nave
of waxed canvas, soft night breeze gently
wafting the triangles as they smelled
the sharp sawdust, floor crunching underfoot

Miners and matrons, crewmen and croppers
poured in to hear the thunder of a God-fearing man
Hiram's face as red as the trumpet vine on Granny's shed
he hollered gospel out strong in 4:4 time
out the nearest canvas like a sail
then flung off his overcoat as John 3:16 spewed forth

He walked, he stomped, he jumped from the pulpit
of a DuPont explosives 50 lb. dynamite box
called sinners out, backsliders too
"Don't stop, don't falter, help folks on down!"
shouted out repentance and future heaven or hell
pressed the righteous to propel sinners up front
to find the holy spirit right there in that dirt

The call was heeded by 17 souls
as plump raindrops bounced off the fabric steeple
offering plates circled around the fresh pine benches
swooping in hard-earned bills like crows at a fest
boys in overalls, girls in flowered jumpers
jingling in their nickels, pennies, dimes
a concluding hymn of *Bringing in the Sheaves*
filtered through holy walls to the house next door
as Preacher Hiram shook hands with exiting folks
his soft flesh dented by honest calloused ones

In the rose-patterned foyer next door, cash changed hands
fielded by Jake, preacher's faithful front man
who had unlatched a tricky lock on the door
and would give you a discount if you gave him a cut
he rested his creaky bones on a ladder back chair,
question down here or up there?

Postlude: Darkness had descended, covering good and bad
Ozone smell provoked by storm, hung in wet air
Hiram could taste it as he padded quietly
in blackness to the house next door
dumped tent revival coffers in a woven bag with the take
then climbed an oak stairway like it was Jacob's ladder
without knocking, barged in his favorite lady's room
Bible still grasped in his hand

JENNIFER BROWNE

In a Period of Absence, She Remembers a Dream

1.
I dream of falling-out teeth.
Throughout the morning,
thoughts of periodontitis,
blood-borne bacteria
blocking arteries, wrecking
valves. I imagine stainless
tools scraping, cleaning out
the chambers of my heart.

2.
You've said the snow has melted
where you are. Where I am, I watch
the snow falling, know a storm
has moved between us, covering.

3.
Having said that I am lonely,
I think of estuaries, changing
color of freshwater-meeting-salt.
Does a line appear where my
vulnerability turns to pathos,
where water blends undrinkable?

4.
The farmer's almanac says
a single crow predicts foul
weather, a crow flying low
brings hard wind. A dark
shape huddles against
bark, the cypress trunk.
The storm calms itself.

5.
vulnerable (adj.)—c. 1600, from Late Latin vulnerabilis "wounding," from Latin vulnerare "to wound, hurt, injure, maim," from vulnus (genitive vulneris) "wound," perhaps related to vellere "pluck, to tear" (see svelte), or from PIE *wele-nes-, from *wele- (2) "to strike, wound" (see Valhalla). also from c. 1600

6.
A dream guide says toothloss
predicts a death in the family.
Another says *jealousy, stress.*
A friend says dreams about
the mouth are about speech,
always crumbling damage
in what we leave unsaid.

7.
To speak with a crow's mouth
is to make the unlucky things
you say happen. I've learned
precognition is just anxiety,
attention, pattern recognition.

8.
Do I say that I am excavating
parts of myself, scraping thin
against time, this absence?

9.
svelte (adj.)—"slender, lithe, fine," 1817, svelt, from French svelte "slim, delicate," (17c.), chiefly a term used in art and architecture, from Italian svelto "slim, slender," originally "pulled out, lengthened," past participle of svellere "to pluck or root out," from Vulgar Latin *exvellere, from Latin ex- "out" (see ex-) + vellere "to pluck, stretch."

10.
I don't know if it is pathos
or vulnerability when I say
I would drive through snow
for half a day to touch you.

11.
We spend the day speaking
about birds. I wait until I know
you've finished what needs saying
to name a collective noun: *unkindness*.

12.
Valhalla (n.)—... first element... from Proto-Germanic *walaz (source also of Old English wæl "slaughter, bodies of the slain," Old High German wal "battlefield, slaughter"), from PIE root *wele- (2) "to strike, wound"... Second element is from höll "hall," from PIE root *kel- (1) "to cover, conceal, save."

13.
I do not know the habits
of the other winter birds,
having closed windows
against them, the cold.
Still, the morning's quiet.
I hear no caw, no croak.

14.
Crows flock. Ravens fly in pairs.

15.
pathos (n.)—"quality that arouses pity or sorrow," 1660s, from Greek *pathos* "suffering, feeling, emotion, calamity," literally "what befalls one," related to *paskhein* "to suffer," *pathein* "to suffer, feel," *penthos* "grief, sorrow;" from PIE root *kwent(h)- "to suffer."

16.
Days later, I remember a sundial
in a garden, the same dream.
I read it is a healing symbol
for the heart, a caution about time.
What will I let myself say?

All etymologies from Online Etymology Dictionary, www.etymonline.com

REBECCA BURGENER

Soar and Pour

dragon dreams and merfolk wishes:
There's more to life than socks and dishes!
"Why can't you stay home, Mama?"

Oh, I pour, and I pour, and I pour, and I pour
—but they want more—
It's natural, I see
I can't expect them, really
to pour back into me

Where do I turn
to refill my cistern?

dragon dreams and merfolk wishes:
Life keeps life-ing between socks and dishes!
"Hold my hand, Mama!"

Let's explore! Let's explore! Let's explore! Let's explore!
—then they let go—
Children, spread your wings
Please fly higher than me
I'm so proud! But with longings

Where do I turn
to refill my cistern?

dragon dreams and merfolk wishes:
I really don't mind the socks and dishes!
"Will you be okay, Mama?"

My prayers soar, and they soar, and they soar, and they soar
—I'm so thankful!—
My children, they grew
Each one builds something new
while I enjoy the view

I know where to turn
to refill my cistern

Thank you, Lord!
For Words

SARAH DIAMOND BURROWAY
Uninvited Guests on a February Morning

In the mess of the renovation, we found strangers.
Dangerous visitors had set up house
in the ceiling of my childhood home.
Sunday morning squatters overhead
near the stove above the kitchen window.
A huge, papery nest, billowed full
like a pan of hot buttermilk biscuits:
whirled, blistery layers crusted at the edge—
its buff color—delicious, mysterious—
brought to mind countless iron skillets
of bubbling grease and milk and flour
that Momma stirred into sausage gravy
to feed us on chilly mornings.
"*Come get you a plate*," she'd call
from the foot of the stairs as we snuggled
deep in the quilted safety of our beds.
But these sleepy hornets are not welcome here.
Not on this chilly mid-winter's day.

KENDALL S. CABLE
Wolf Full Moon

Words sculpted by inspired lips
Waft like incense
Smoky, lingering
Incantations, spells
Of truth and magic
Summoning gods and goddesses
From the celestial
As Eros shakes rose petals from his hair and
Aphrodite awakens from a dreamy slumber
In a gown full of stars
To gaze upon the spectacle this twilight
Of candlelight flicker against shadow
As muses sway in corners
To the rhythm of the poetic
Spinning stories like wispy webs
Rendering prey
Spellbound and enchanted
Under the silver shimmer of the Wolf Full Moon

JILLIAN CALAHAN
Forbidden

You feel forbidden.
A fruit so sweet
my teeth ache
at the thought of
you between them.
I salivate rivers
just holding your name
on my tongue.
And when you smile,
my soul contracts
beneath my core.
A pulling, pulsing ache
that takes my breath away.
And oh the rapids,
the white water honey
and the way it drips
just for you.
I would burn
all of Eden down
just to taste you.
Bury my face in
the pith of your neck.
Break my teeth
on the pit.

SAM CALHOUN
Winter Solstice 2024

Having written the solstice early,
having nothing left to write about
save the cadence of the dog's breath
moving the bed sheet in asemic ripples,
so sound asleep she misses the sirens,
the ambulatory rush of December winds
toying the rose hips rising through the
berry-less hollies beneath the streetlight,
how every door of every room here, safe,
closed, becomes a kind of eclipse, a nightlight
corona creeping the pink dawn, saying be here,
the days growing like moss on maples.

NECIA CAMPBELL
Lyric Handshake, a Friendship Ghazal

Eclectic group, all strangers at the start, attend Kim's words,
commit a year to poetry and now, as friends, spin words.

Nostalgia and a razor wit's insight to pastime fun
bring life to ghosts of Yankees past—a love redreamt in words.

Somewhere outside the Midwest city sprawl, a broken, long-
retired girl whose strength speaks through her trauma lens pimps words.

A single strand of sticky silk, though delicate, entraps;
strong images that dot her dew-kissed web transcend limned words.

Loud rumble; white-hot flash—a poem etched in sand, now glass,
is sharp and burrowed deep—her stormcloud genius vents grim words.

Displaced, a seed of prairie grass observes the wind-blown plains,
collecting bird's-eye images; she now descends with words.

Melodious in gentle breezes, alloyed notes resound,
their soft-chimed song a soothing balm for others' spread-thin words.

This humble fool's a realist that bares her soul in rhyme—
the proffered piece my lyric handshake—I'm extending words.

NANCY CAPRANICA CARLSON
On Becoming God

Take a bite;
I dare you.
I swear
it's delicious.
The story, the prose,
It's sanctimonious purpose.
Meant to scare you,
press you,
into submission.
But you.
You don't subscribe
to that fiction.
Take a bite,
I insist.
The plot,
well it thickens.
Full of twists and twirls,
and intricate lessons,
full of words and wonder,
and petulant girls
who ate, but never sickened.
It's an utter lie.
The knife, the spoon
the fork
in the tongue
of the one
who started it all.
With his belly crawl,
slithery come
hither my child and eat.
Take a bite and see
what he offered
was Truth.
The most delicious fruit,
that smacks
of beauty, of pain,

of love, of lust,
of thirst, of touch,
trepidation, elation,
unforgivable joy,
unending question.
The most exquisite stuff:
the mouth feel of knowledge.
The power, the proof,
that sits on the tongue,
dying to be swallowed.
Everyone knows,
that Eve knew,
exactly what she was given.
And she should have kept it hidden, all to herself.
But instead
she was
oddly driven
to present
that ribald rib-giver,
that primordial pea,
a chance at something original.
(We women have always been generous, generous to a fall.)
And in one juicy slurp
mankind was birthed
and would rule
in perpetuity.
She asked, "what will they do to me?"
Sweet woman, you have no idea.

DIANE CARMONY

The Office of Dr. W.D. Hutchings (Madison, Indiana)

Bottles of concoctions and medicines
are carefully lined up in rows
mirroring the daughter's photographs,
the ones she took on the day he died.

This is the world of a smalltown doctor
and the tools of the trade in the 1800s:
forceps for childbirth,
pliers for pulling teeth,
the jagged edge of a bone saw.

Here it comes to life,
the daily work of a dedicated physician:
50 cents to extract a tooth,
50 dollars to amputate a leg.

Payment is accepted in cash or kind:
books, corn, apples
and perhaps
a painting or two.

C.A. CARPENTER
The Last Day

On the last day,
will I see only
the imperfections?

   Rue the incomplete?
   Grieve the lost?
   Regret the unmet?

On the last day,
Will I finally find
The strength to drop the weight?

   Allow a softening?
   Release the grip?
   But not give up?

On the Last Day
Will I find the wisdom
to count the kindnesses?

   Welcome the new?
   Clear the desk?
   Begin Again?

MARY CARTER

How to Exhume an Old Woman from 1450

1. Strip away the topsoil with a spade, noting the color. As soon as the color changes, stop and switch tools to a hand trowel.
2. Carefully, using the trowel, remove the next layer until you notice the color changing indicating there has been a disturbance. The darker soil is probably the grave site.
3. Now switch to a wooden popsicle stick. Using a scooping motion, continue removing the soil.
4. Coffin wood or the forehead of the skull will protrude before anything else.—Unless the ground was farmed. In that case, notice the skulls will be flattened from the heavy farm equipment rolling over the graves.
5. Using the popsicle stick, scoop the soil away from the bone. If the bone surface is moist or wet, spritz often with water, to maintain that moisture level.
6. You may allow the sand or soil to dry on the protuberance so it can be more easily brushed away. But after that, moisten the bone surface again with water.
7. As the layers are removed, other bones can be handled in this order:
    a. Major long bones of legs and arms
    b. Collar bones, vertebrae, and ribs (which will be flattened)
    c. Hands and feet
8. Note the following features:
    a. the last three lumbar vertebrae are fused together, indicating great amount work bending and lifting.
    b. Lower mandible had started to be reabsorbed after loss of teeth.
    c. Lack of bone sutures indicating no broken bones
    d. Hardly any arthritic lipping on the bones of hands

Untold:
Bodies bathed.
Clothes washed by hand and wrung out.
Clothes hung on clotheslines.
Vegetables gathered.
Wood for kindling gathered.
Babies birthed, nursed, and/or buried.
Children nurtured.
Food washed, cut, cooked, and thrown out.

Stories told.
Teeth pulled.
Hair tucked under scarves.
Shirts buttoned.
Hands brushed against skirts to dry.
Eyes squinted to watch approaching weather.
Faces washed.
Glances shared.
Whispered words.

JENN CAVANAUGH
Futility

Language fails once again
assigning such a Noble
Word to the sense
that Everything
you're Doing
is Being
Un-

Oh, but it's a defiant failure
to Name it so finely

An acute act of re-
Sistance this in-
Sistence that
Meaning may be
Made in spite and in
Service of its
Own transience

F utility

In this hour
Between storms
I shall gather leaves
With no illusion of once
And for all arranging them
For the benefit of others
Walking into the wind

Make of them what you will

DELA COLEMAN-POSEY
Quiet

Air thick with anger, confusion, despair,
fear, pain, resignation.

The tray table is crowded.
Blow Pops, cranberry juice,
a teddy bear holding a heart.

A ZZZZZZZZZZZTING fly,
trapped between white blinds
and window jambs, is loud.

Memories become distant—rending
relationships between life/death,

while the reaper waits, for the one
still/writhing sleep/waking,
facing future.

The turnstile into the void
awaits each watcher too,
without exception

TIM CONROY
Bloodstone

For Carol

The stone-colored door of her walk-up
At my sister's East Village Apartment
Above the smell of curry
Above a street that's a river
That murmurs with current
Over more stones
Over the stream of decades
Each encounter rippling
Winding her around city blocks
Flowing with stones that fit
Agate, slate, river rocks
Into the tightest spaces
Into the mosaic of colors
Into the babbling city
Hardened by something elusive
By something that wears
A painful, rural past
Of misogyny and abuse
With a stone in her palm
Tumbling to the next bend
With book vendors
Ordering a bagel
Chattering on the Highline
With visiting siblings
Who feel like sediment
By the cascading rocks
Our bloodstone surges ahead
Until found dead by her tub
A rock never pocketed

MARGARET COOMBS

February Program on the Birds of Costa Rica

Jewel tones pop against cloud forest
greenery. Blue-crowned Motmot.
Crimson-backed Tanager. We're tutored

on the Resplendent Quetzal, whose tail
feathers guided princes, augured futures,
plumed beauties. Caribbean views, yellow

rumps, yellow pantaloons, attractive
as Mardi Gras dancers. Clay-colored
Thrushes, Yellow-throated Toucans.

Here's another sexy bird. We ooh
at the Green Kingfisher's saturated plumage.
This one knocked me out. The audience

agrees. The warm orange of the Cinnamon
Hummingbird. Now our sweaters feel hot.
Someone passes out bird-friendly chocolates.

People smile at each other. It's Valentine's Day.
At sight of the Violet-Crowned Woodnymph,
I reach for my partner's hand. I just fell in love.

SUSAN MICHELE CORONEL
Wish

There were no crickets in the hedges,
only velvet green cake, smooth & slippery
as algae. I wanted a holy birthday
with shamrocks, to channel the luck
of the Irish. My god, how I craved it—
a system to keep safe, to track glowing
thoughts that emerged out of nowhere
but needed a home in the world. Not ambiguous,
but clear as a bluegrass band—banjo & fiddle
notes sliding across hardwood floors.
As cool as a fish on my belly in summer—
no menace, no heartbreak—just green
mowed lawns as I lay down, earthworms
excavating ground without malice or weeds.

LISA COTTRELL
What Age Did You Realize Death?

What age did you first realize death
not as if they had just moved away
like the great grandmother
with whom you were not close
who was so old it was not a surprise

What age did you realize death
not like the complete shock and disbelief
of your beloved uncle's suicide
when you were too young to bear it
and tucked the pain away

What age did you realize death
of someone you loved
like your witty gay friends
who all were worn to bone by AIDS
who trembled at the specter of death

What age did you realize death
of a very dear friend or loved one
a child or spouse and feel
your heart ripped to shreds
and dripping everywhere you go

What age did you realize death
would be coming for you
yes, you. Really.
whether you expect it or not
whether you are young or old
or somewhere in the middle

What age did you realize
you will lose it all
all you have
all you are
everyone and everything you love

What age did you realize
life is fleeting and precious
learn to choose wisely
and always say I love you
when you see the ones you love

What age did you realize life
and death

Or have you yet

CATHREN COUGILL

Sorry It's Been a While

Sorry it's been a while
since I showed up
on the date
for our date.
I think about you
every day, imagining
how this relationship
could really progress…

But it's the time
it's the attention
it's the detail and
intention.
It's getting into
the right head space or
getting out of my head—
or maybe a little of both?

And finding or choosing
the right words to express my
heart—ache—experience—desire
in a casual, deliberate, intelligent, ardent,
understandable, and purposeful voice—
My Voice.

It's creating the habit, but
not too much habit that
sameness or rigidity sets in.
Just how do we make
time without allowing
time to take over?
How do we hold
spontaneity, spark, and creativity
alongside rhythm, routine, and plan?

How can all of this
coexist and create opportunity
for authentic expression and connection?

Cheers to the date, our date, and to your hospitality.

GLENDA COWEN-FUNK
Fault Lines

I've heard predictions since elementary school—//
Any day the New Madrid Fault will //
erupt in a cataclysmic event. //
Its prolific intraplate earthquakes //
rattle our world along Old Man River. //
Future eruptions could split the midwest along its river highway, but //
we already live in a land of seismic divisions. //
A fissure opened along party fault lines. //
Political tectonic plates shifted & erupted in //
cataclysmic chaos of unmeasurable magnitude. //
Structures buckle under the tremor's force. //
Whether geological or political fault lines, //
a nation erupting against itself gets buried in //
Pompeii's same rubble.

BARBARA CRARY
Play/Ground

The constant seesaw,
The pendulum's swing,
The playground in my mind
teeters on the brink of manic
dispare

Its ground littered with
candy wrappers and remains
of brown soda in scuffed
plastic bottles, holdovers
from sweeter days.

I have to believe that
I'll feel better if I clean this up.

But what if I leave the playground
with no sign of life? What remains?
The seesaw static/the swings stilled.
If there is no movement here, is there
a point to the play?

COLETTE CROWN
Humans Can Be Museums

Dry, dusty bones
Malinger under
Layers of sediment.

Someday they will
Delight the archaeologist
Who unearths them.

They will tell the story
Of a different
Time and place.

An era of exuberance
That crashed and burned,
Leaving nothing but

Ashes and bones.

KARLA DANIEL
Courage

My words morphed into images unknown,
Bizarre markers of wisdom obscured.
How to see clearly this life being lived?
Have courage!
Trust to your passions,
Cosmic cycles, stars at night,
Daytime light.
Count on basics
To see you set right.
Have courage!

LAURA DANIELS
Dagger

She drops the dagger into the ditch.
Doesn't she know it will be found?
Like a thief, she steals away.

She escapes evidence with ease.
Everywhere she turns, she is open.
Like a thief, she steals away.

She flies into the forest like a fugitive.
Faraway, she feels safe sanctuary.
Like a thief, she steals away.

JEANICE EAGAN DAVIS
I Have Wasted My Life

Title from "Lying in a Hammock at William Duffy's Farm in Pine Island, Minnesota" by James Wright

and so too have I
forgetting too often
there is more
than the small
bird, grey and plain
to turn my gaze upon

or even the red bird
bright as berries
or the blue bird
swathed in the sea

or the floating clouds
ordinary, expected
I fail to remember
how little the sun
rising matters

or its setting
I overlook that rain falls
birds sing, trees sigh
that the green of days
always returns to gold
to grey

LEE DESROSIERS

Uses for a Stick

Since humanity was new
humans used sticks
to transport fire before
the famous trick with
a stick, some kindling
to bring forth spark.
Sharpened a lot of sticks
before discovering the match
small but powerful enough
to start a forest fire, made
pointed sticks to attach
a sharpened stone.
When not fighting, made
flutes out of bamboo,
bassoons of hardwood,
bows for violins and cellos,
batons for conductors and
cheerleaders, fancy drum sticks
paddles for canoes, masts
for sailboats, fishing rods.
With the advent of metallurgy
forged swords, guns, cooking
and building tools, plastic
gave us car parts
such as stick shifts,
canes and prosthetic legs,
table legs, knives
forks, spoons, chopsticks,
bobby pins, pins, needles
for sewing, needles for
medicine, other medical
sticks like stents, tongue
depressors, surgical tools
for various sticking
and the tape to stick
the sticks with.

TAMERA NEILSON DOBBINS
Health and Time Are Life's Treasure

Illness is stealthy.
Unexpectedly stealing
away health and energy.
Stopping time
before we're able
to treasure
last moments
we thought were
just another day.
We're never ready
to say goodbye,
and tears like rain,
can't heal hearts
they left behind.

BRANWEN DREW
The New Year

Act now to save the future.
Beware of threats to democracy.
Change for the better will come.
Disdain for the humanity of the other is rampant.
Events appear beyond our control.
Future is uncertain.
Gratitude for each other must be shown,
Hatred cannot be condoned.
Individuals must stand as one against tyranny.
Justice for all is paramount.
Know that we must fight for equal rights.
Love will overcome hatred.
Mount meaningful actions against bigotry.
Never give up hope.
Overt action must be taken.
Priorities include community and stewardship.
Queue up to help the needy.
Reach out across chasms of misunderstanding.
Seek peace and tranquility.
Truth speaks louder than lies.
Understanding each other is needed.
Victory of democracy over fascism is our goal.
When to act is now.
Xenophobic ideas are wrong.
Yearn for peace, love, and equality.
Zest for life and love will keep us going.

BARBARA EDLER
Snow

Snow erases

      Mother's name

           Joy and spring

WHISPER EDWARDS

An Ache that Never Thaws

I miss the winters I've never known—
the quiet hush, the cold of moonlit snow.

I confess to the hollow,
shivering walls,
to a hearth that's a tomb
where warmth once stayed.
A ghost lost in a house of bare echoes,
yearning for a winter
that could carry my name.

Outside, the trees stand like broken veins,
their branches frayed, fists raised
to a shadowed sky.

If only I had lived through frost's slow decay,
I'd know what it is to stand stripped, exposed—
yet rooted, silent, in the weight of cold.

Stars here do not promise;
they dim and drift,
hollow as vows that never reached flame.

And the chill I yearn for is more than air—
it's the cold where memory takes shape,
where snow holds silence like a buried truth.

I ache for the frost that never split my skin,
for the sharp crack
of branches bearing unseen phantoms.

These nights feel empty,
hollowed of winter's weight—
and I'm left here, longing
for a silence, a snow,
that might name what's missing
beneath my skin.

AALIYAH EL-AMIN
A Plate of Grief

Grateful for the laughter of relatives, despite clipped exchanges, smiling
while evading hollow eye contact.

Curious cousins, whose fathers are still here,
not knowing the right words to say.

Bringing baskets of food to sit until cold atop counters already filled with
three casseroles, along with a carved roast to be heated when they return.

Yet, my plate remains empty, even with food,
still empty. Steady drip of tears pooling until
sealing my lips shut.

Craving to intake water to escape its parchedness.

Sinking in a sea of blackness repelling any gestures of love—suspended,
engulfed by mourning, still drowning.

Checkered panes become my eyes' safe resting place. Staring at the last
blackberries hanging around the fence line.

While the sunset's harmony graces the horizon, loosening its embrace to
the quiet chill of nightfall.

Stillness is interrupted by a dying orange meteor procession lighting the
sky, as my heart bursts and grief spills out.

Crawling to the fridge at 2am, ravenously filling my mouth, trying to
hold on to any bit of you left,
long past your repast.

LESLIE ENZIAN
The Privacy of Them

The air surrounding their forested grove
Formed insulated, sound-proof walls
Only sounds of
whispered confidences
permitted

There was no Before, no After
No Outside
No Others

Just a melding of souls
Alchemy of honey flowing through sap
Synergistically potent concoction
More sweet than either alone

As they gazed into
Shadowed depths of pools,
Margins of each obscuring,
They wondered if there
Was a bottom
Or fathomless depths
to spelunk for eternity

From the ripples
Sun sparks ricocheted
Burned patterns on retinas
Imprinting the bond

Ineffable, gut-level tremors
Resonated in synchrony
Their superimposed sine waves
Of a frequency
Heretofore unknown

Understanding
In all ITS fullness
Seeing each with telescopic clarity

Such was the gravity
of union
That the surrounding cosmos
Pulled inwards,
spiraling around the pair

The whole of the Universe
Condensing on the head of a pin—
A reversed Big Bang
All things sucked across the
Event Horizon
Swallowed into a black hole
That only they floated beyond

KARIN EVANS
Dark Waters

Ready to help the young boy
with his writing, I sit down
in the kid-sized chair, smile at him,
and wait. He smooths his paper

with both palms and reads softly
what he has written for a class assignment
about a favorite memory. This is his:
A hot day in the summer

when his daddy took him fishing
at a lake, a lake with dragonflies.
They sat together on the bank,
drank cold lemonade, and dropped

their lines. "My daddy's gone now,"
he whispers. "He went away
and I don't think he's ever coming back.
I'd do anything to find him."

He slides the paper toward me.
"That must be so hard," I say.
He nods silently, looks down, and waits
for me to help him fix

the grammar and the spelling,
his pencil now a fishing pole
clenched above dark waters.

R.G. EVANS
Grace Notes

The church organist would play
the last line of the hymn's refrain
then linger   on a final note,
one long invitation to our ears,
our tongues, our very souls
to join the party all together
as one voice lifted in tune
to rise through the rafters
and please our Lord.

Was He pleased with our cacophony
of sharps and flats, our tin-eared syncopation,
or with our thousand thoughts
of lust and wrath, of things both venal and mortal
that blocked our prayers like river dams,

or was it enough, the accidental unity
of sound once or twice a hymn
when all our voices converged
on a single perfect note that hung in the air
like Christ on the cross, what we could give
in place of our lives to please Him,
a moment's grace whether we deserved it or not?

HELENA FAGAN
Disquiet

In the night they steal my sleep,
fill my days with tremors—
moths that ride the blood in my veins,
thrumming, tiny, hammers.

Once some golden moths,
so tiny I was unaware,
wintered in a glass-fronted cabinet,
fed on the braided hair

of my Eskimo dolls,
feasted on rabbit fur of mukluks
my daughter wore as a child,
left the skin exposed and bare.

Devoured all the fox fur
cuffing my sealskin mitts,
left large drifts of golden wings
that disintegrated at my touch.

How help my inner moths escape,
leave my blood to itself,
how keep from turning
to piles of golden dust?

ANNA FINCH
Our Voices

Our voices,
Can be small,
Can be gregarious,
I have tried to be both.
I get upset when I don't share my voice.
I also get upset when I share it too much—
So, the balance is needed as in everything.
To listen to the inner nudge when it is the right time to share,
And when it's the right time to listen.
I do believe we help and encourage each other when we share our voices—
A blend of different experiences and wisdom.
So, I do love listening to others sharing their voices.
And I think others like to hear mine as well.
To share with love as my friend Cherise said—
Without fear of judgement,
Authentically us.
To bring more unconditional love to the world,
Just by sharing our voices.
It's the small things that have the biggest impact sometimes.

MARY EICHHORN FLETCHER
Beaver Moon, Midnight

"Do not be afraid, for I am with you." Isaiah 41:10

In the still of this night
with its hard cold air
when the moon waxes larger
(and largest yet)
(strange signs)
and the last of the four
(super)moons has marched in
in a row
and the silence is filled
with treachery and omens
of what is
(or perhaps is)
to come.

It is then that
I listen for the loons
and the lake
and the heliotrope
(so recently passed)
to sing their sad songs
and croon their sweet perfumes
and sigh
their long sighs.

And the sighs of this moon
and this lake
and this night
and the keens of the dark
purple flower
make me long now,
for the softness of spring
and not to tremble in fear.

JUDITH-KATE FRIEDMAN
Beyond the Ballet

By time I was eight
so much had turned upside down.
Daddy had flown on
before Mother's Day
five weeks after MLK.
RFK followed.

I asked the rooftops:
Why is everyone dying?
The streetlamp flickered.
I asked the asphalt.
I asked the ailanthus.
They had no answers.

Then color streamed in
breaking through Chagall's windows
at Lincoln Center.
My aunt insisted
that we take in this beauty
beyond the ballet.
There we stood, in awe
bathed in light's shifting splendors,
the whole world present.

When I came back home,
my mom was in the kitchen
concocting magic.
Viennese crescents
rolled out, shaped, devotedly
dusted with sugar.

Something old and new
gracing her face as they baked.
A rare tenderness.
Recipes survive.
Antidotes to bitterness,
sweeter with each bite.

TAMMY FORNER

Climate Change

New snow—just the second good snow this winter,
surprisingly deep on limbs of dogwood.
Fingerling branches fist up, grasp soft cotton bolls.
Agile grey juncos skate off when trying to alight.
        This makes me laugh out loud.

I look across my small front yard,
street and houses beyond
gathered in grove of elderly pines
that hoard drifts of white, aloft
until wind passes through—
        and they *phluph!* their bounty on my head.

Once, my view was stream and rock wall
parting white-blanketed, rolling farmhouse lawn.
Connecticut woods. So many snow days.
Two small boys, and ancient red barn
where sleds were stabled in anticipation.
        No cares, just joy—and hills to slide down.

Today, I feel the loss.

So rare, these deep white days have become.
I struggle to shake the winds of why.
No bounty—this burden falls hard,
lands on heart and mind, damping wonder-light
        and yet—for today—wonder returns.

"My candle burns, not to dispel the darkness,
        but to put forth the Light."[1]

The cause is not changed.
I am simply reminded of what is lost, more often.

---

[1] Quote from the photograph on my desk, by author and photographer, Charlie Siegel, grandson of writer Bernie Siegel, Simsbury, CT.

To weather this age, I must dwell
in the beauty of re-membering,
sing again the joy of every deep snowy day,
the antics of small winter birds, and grandmother trees.

Allow the Light of it to restore the climate in my soul.

CMARIE FUHRMAN
Between Desire and Expectation

So this is the canyon I am meant to live
in. It's walls of different countries.
And what of that river that carved it?
This is where Jung chimes in, *silly girl*
the river is you. The river is life
the river is your subconscious. And I
believe this in the same way I believe June.
Yet, I feel like I am more island, just off
center. Upon me are the comings
and goings of deer and turkey vultures—
sometimes the footprints of men.
Isn't an island just land that lost
it's mother? Somewhere, below all this
consciousness, roots still hold,
or maybe granite, something stabilizing,
connecting. I know nothing
about floating islands, so I believe
I have already chosen a side,
that deep down, I understand my legacy
as something that not only I,
but all of you can see
and abandon me to as well.

KATHLEEN FULLERTON
The Space Between

I bid you goodbye
in the space between life and heartbreak

A cold winter fog is our shroud
yet birds feast
of red berries on the bare limbed current.

Rain pelts the windows
yet our forlorn fallow garden fills
with rivulets of nature's tears, hope

Fat wet drops bejewel lichen covered branches
yet sedate patient trees
while away
as I will too
this winter's weary burden.

I must bid you goodbye
yet know I will have you always
in this space between

TRINA GAYNON

Pharaohs, Carpenters, and Leafcutters

An ant devours...
   "Ants and Sharks," Tomasz Różycki

I don't know who you think made the world. Word is, it was the ants. Ants carve a path. Their march is coordinated. Each ant follows the next. They chant, *We must change the earth*. The mantra today is the same as yesterday.

They smell their enemies coming. They hold grudges. Sting. Bite. Pinch. A row of ants battles through heat and humidity, trekking across the cracked sidewalks. They follow the scent of all that is sweet.

The peony beckons. Be careful if you take this flower into your house. So many ants feeding there, herding and milking aphids. Yet you will only see one or two at a time. The crepe myrtle beckons. There are a thousand ants living inside. But only one or two will tumble from a vase onto the table. Any one of them could find a crack in the invisible, be a messenger of the holy.

CATHY GEORGE
We the People

Almost everyone on the train is kind.

Can I help you lift that?
Will you watch my bag while I...
Do you want anything from the café car?
I'll make this call short, promise.

Rummaging for ear buds
our eyes meet we bond over the annoying volume
that person speaks at

Over the loudspeaker our conductor tangles his words
laughs at himself
we laugh with him

Not knowing who voted for whom
We the people momentarily get along—
Knowing we are divided and cut-throat

The train barrels onward
God's clanging cradle rocks back and forth
lulling us in voter anonymity

For a moment
up the Eastern seaboard
differences that make oneness unimaginable

briefly dissolve
we share the same destination
hoping to arrive whole

FRED GERHARD

The End of a Sonnet Is Not the End of the Poem

After Jamaica Baldwin's American sonnet,
"The End of Sorrow Is Not Happiness"

Would you believe me if I told you the
end of the sonnet was in these two lines,
up front, instead of at the couplet we
have been trained to expect to turn in rhyme?

The sonnet-sized heart is brimful with ends
like mourning dove mornings on fluted wings.
To arrive at a sonnet's hovering pen,
something somewhere sings or stings.

For what dissolves and sets began as dawn,
and who resolves to get it down in words
must ache with endings at the first drawn
line, then wait for beginnings—how absurd,

the couplet contrived at its birth to end
right here, where the sonnet begins again.

TANYA GOGO
Rising

Rubble on the ground again
smoke rising from ashes and stone
I survey, assess
two bricks fell side by side
or maybe clung to each other
while their world fell
I place another stone, then another
beside, behind, above them until
destruction becomes my platform
and falling fuels my rising

RENATA GOLDEN

Jane

Of course I stayed in the jungle
with him. Nineteen and unused
to the logic of bad mistakes
I succumbed.

Up close that warmth
filled my future like I owned it.
My story written by men
blind to their own omissions
their wimpy imaginations.

You know how it is.
Pretty young with stars
in my eyes, all the life boats broken.

I never missed my life back home
wedding parties, funeral hymns
parents who named me
after that other woman
who also had a thing for apes.
She thought she was better than me.
Everyone knows both her names.

Everyone knows me because a man
had never seen a woman before.
Everyone knows all things were primitive
in those days in the jungle.

BECKY GOODWIN
Oh, Possibility!

Oh, Possibility,
I dwell in thee!
You are where I live.
To thee my life I give.
In thee, I am home,
Wherever I roam.
You are the Light within.
You are the Healing for all that's been.
You are the Pulse of the sea.
You are the Heart of me.

ALI GRIMSHAW
Belief in Planting

As I dig deeply down to tuck you in safely, one by one, in softness, grounded for growth with care and wishes for your survival. (Awareness of my lack of qualifications and experience crowd into the activity like a boisterous neighbor who wasn't invited. "This won't work. You don't know what you're doing.")

As I put my shovel away, I am thinking about internal resistance. My resistance to planting, to bothering with placing all of you in the earth. My head saying, "You're doing it wrong. You will be disappointed." My heart replying, "Let's try. I need to wonder."

Now I am pondering, curious actually, what would it be like to live without a belief in planting. Realizing I already know. I have been there and don't want to go back.

I am seeding a future I cannot see. I am planting hope in the dark cold of winter. This includes garlic cloves and my belief in loving action to grow the next. Stepping into the unknowable with a curious heart that knows it doesn't always work out and planting it anyway.

Later that day I found three more cloves in my pocket. Three that escaped planting day. Their potential is not lost. I will find time to tuck them into bed too.

Cover them with leaves.

With gratitude,

Ali Grimshaw

SUSAN HAIFLEIGH
Waiting for Grace

To be alive is an obscuring grace.
This world, too burdened,
harsh remains.

The young cannot escape a fate
set in motion before their parents
were ever born.

To see what cannot be seen,
to watch what cannot be borne, no choice
when choice is gone.

Empty containers for the lost march
across distant dirty fields, each mourned
without a place to stop or settle down.

Barren vessels on empty altars bear witness
to their absent remains, huddling, umbrellas
lifted to rain, we wait for grace.

EMILIA HALEY
Sounds Depicted from a Monday Afternoon

noises
clatter
bang
chatter
none of which
I merge into
so I don't
make
a sound
at all

JONATHAN HALL

Perspective

Having me sit as Truth
While you mark my every line and curve
In cold, unblinking detail is
One thing.
But, then, to force me
From this solitary study
Into the closet of your mind
Frantically searching for
Some beautiful, flowery address
To cover me up with just
So you can present me, to the public,
As a palatable, yet provocative silhouette?

Well, it's winter out there and our mind closet's full of parkas.

So, no.

We don't feel like being a poet today.

KATHERINE HANCOCK
Winter

Today everything sleeps, buried
away from the cold.
      Buried in our own thoughts.
      Buried to give our seeds purchase.

The way a seed carries a tree within it, we
hold and begin,
      root, branch, leaf and flower.
The order of our movement,
a million years becoming.
      We breathe the dark dampness of mother.
      We hold the paradox of living and dying.

Your politics mean nothing.
      You need to know the river.
           Listen to the breeze.
Become the leaf through its life from
form to element.

Fall naked into the stream.
Become earth, water, sun.
      Become life falling
      into life.

MJ HATFIELD
Petrichor

A part of me still
is there on that hill, in all
moss, rocks, slate, fern leaves,
with the dirt that covers the
dead's eyes. The wet spice
of wild onion;
knuckles deep in black, fragrant earth.
My palm covers acorns
with dirt like how you close the
dead's eyes. Let them grow
among unkempt grass, garden,
the home where they both once lived.
A part of me still
is there on that hill, in all.
Rain falls a curtain
of silk strands on moss, rocks, slate,
fern leaves, wild onion, unkempt grass,
garden, acorns, against gray land
framed by the windowpane in
the home where they both once lived.
Oh, let me gather those thin
drops as if the clouds were worms.

CHRISTINE HAVENS
Short Serenade for Putty and Strings

Silly Putty
    Silly Putty
stretched & pulled
    p u l l e d   &   s t r e t c h e d
snap
right
back

zing
        zing
                zing
I'd
rather
be
Silly
String

MELISSA HELTON
(Re)Forest

I took an ax to my idea of what my heart should be
and accepted what it was. After it dried, I split
that brittle pulp and put it to the flames.
I hover near the heat of past dreams,
warm my hands, then nap quietly,
alone. Those newly divorced
from the future they burned
sleep heavily, solid, deep,
away from all their
remorse, guilt
and anger.

In that dream-space of flaring winter,
in 4:00 slanting light, pre-solstice,
I breathe with the mountains, their
core older than the evolution of bones.

And I ask the cold
stones exactly what
will sprout from the space
I just clearcut. Me again? Or
an overrun of eager invasives?
A hunting road? A Dollar General? What
will be here after? The microcosm of human
vision is shorter than this old hickory's, which is
shorter than the withering mountain's, which is shorter
still than the arcing stars' that will diligently return tonight
to spark the new-moon-sky dark while we gather to ask ourselves

again and again what we can possibly do.

HALEY HNATUK
A Haunting

For William "Bill" Hnatuk

I woke up
and suddenly the leaves are falling
it's October
and even though you aren't here—you are everywhere

You are the three decaf coffee pods on the side of my countertop
the late-growing cucumber that appeared in my balcony garden
the light shining from my Alexa ready to tell me some new arbitrary thing

You are the voices of the Phillies' fans on the streets yesterday
screaming for Red October

Your voice still echoes in my head
the thought that it might fade hurts more than the haunting does

BOB HOEPPNER
Wake

A blurred hurry of hurting light
breaks open the head of the sleeper.
Like an egg, the skull cracks open to day.
The bird of the brain opens an eye like a beak,
gaping for food, fuel for the feathers of thought
to fluff and ruffle and try to fly.
If premature, there is a fall from the foliage
of pride, flightless, flailing, feathers fouled
from grit on the ground. Goo
from new mud of muddled opinions
shaped from yesterday's news
screw through the fuses of flowers
blooming in shades of truth,
from which I pick for me, and you for you.

JONATHAN HORWITZ
The Choice

This morning the Sun came up
over the hill, and my mind wandered
back to then when we made things
of earth, grass, wood, stone, skin,
there was no escaping the moment,
it was right now, no matter what,
no box to open with laughing fools,
no polluting chariot to drive
over the horizon.
Our stone age ancestors did not worry
if the world would last until Sunset,
or if some old man, younger than I am,
would push a button
and close the door forever.
Come back, now, to this moment,
reach out, take the child you are
by the hand, and stride
into the new day knowing
that we are alive, the choice to live—
and how we do it—is ours.
Do not hesitate to take
your next step into life

ROBERT HUGHES
Jean Vigo

Help me to see clearly because I'm running out of time —Maktub

Son of an anarchist with a fugitive childhood
and given another name as a boarding student
where repression turned into victorious rebellion
against oppressive absurdity with *Zero for Conduct*

On tubercular time ticking in a city armed with a camera
and Vertov's brothers; urban rhythms sculpted
and explored with cinematic possibilities
More than a film *about* Nice, this was *their* Nice

Next, he is with *Taris*, the champion in a natatorium
Here Vigo, is in full dynamic pursuit of this aquatic master
exploring all means of space time and perspective
both above and, inevitably, underwater with him

And in *L'Atlante* true love was confirmed
with moments of transcendent poetry
that point to possibility of other sublime moments
he would not be able to deliver, but instead would inspire
generations pursuing dreams of their own

MARIE LINDE HUSBY
Writer's Block

What is writer's block?
I'm curious to find out
I put down my pen
and stare out the window
Trying to think of absolutely nothing
The greyish winter weather must be
perfect for this
Nothing to see
The empty piece of paper
The lonely pen
surprisingly inviting
Actively standing still
moves me
and the pen

SHELLI HUTCHINSON
In the Beginning

1.17.24

Time stopped in Portland today.
The sky rained ice, covering the trees in a glossy cellophane.
Buds poking from the ground froze in place.
Breath, visible in the frigid air, hung in suspense,
Or maybe anticipation.
Harken creation.
Pen to paper.
First drafts.
Vulnerable.
Grateful.
Shehecheyanu, v'kiy'manu, v'higiyanu laz'man hazeh.
For giving us life, for sustaining us and for allowing us to reach this season.
A celebration of the new, each day a first.
Beginning.

MARY IMO-STIKE
Be Here with Me

Be here with me, Sharon Olds
help me strip away the pretense
you predicted for my female days
ground down into seed for sowing.

Help me embrace
the truth about my animal life,
habitual, sparked by dawns and darknesses,
comfortably generational
let it satisfy me, too.

I never was a mother in your sense
but my womb asked for life
before they sucked it out
now is just an old story
I tell myself past midnight,
instead of dreams.

Count me as your sister, Sharon Olds,
chasing meaning in the same places
this doughy flesh I kneel before
a female Buddha.
I bring to your party all I have,
All I have.

CYNTHIA JACOBI
Orderliness

I don't know you, Bill, and you don't know me
but I know we have walked the same path
for we were thrust into a club
where no parent wants membership.

It's in the wrong order for a parent to outlive their child.
It should be thus:
First—the river, then the ocean.
First—the chicken, then the egg.
First—the omelette—then the newspaper.
First—the headlights, and the swerve, then the fawn.

People may ask, "How are you?"
I say I am alive and keep moving along our path.

HOLLY JAHANGIRI
Throwaway Planet

In searching for the words
to make apologies
to trees, for every crumpled
draft, it's clear that some
see Earth as flawed; instead
of edits, they would toss
it all; incinerate
us in the blazing sun
believe a better page
awaits, on other worlds
light years, lifetimes, away.

NANCY JENTSCH
Snow and Soil

Let me whirr into the new year—
a top spinning above immaculate

snow fields—leaving the rages of past
years as embers whose ash will soon

be as white and cold as the snow,
the snow that awes in its freshness—

each flake glittering like a sought-after
gem. The ashes—matte and dull—

will find their bloom as well, seeping
with time into soil, soil they nurture

with echoes of past fury's flames.

KIM JOHNSON
Mornings in Eden

it must have
seemed silly
a half century
ago, all those groggy
early morning meccas
padding barefooted ~ a
young bedheaded takhaar
to the clink-keeping rhythms
of classic-fringed frippery
into the kitchen
a young Nastaliq-quest seeker
of Ottoman culture
too underripe for my
I Dream of Jeannie
baggy-panted harem
hajjah jammies
still, sleep-savvy
with a meadow-winked
pink and red chiffon
belly-dancer bra top: me
pulling a chair
to the oven
offering my
skinny feet
to the revved-up broiler's heat
spilling out from
the open door
after the buttered waffles
but that's how freezing
little barefooted
1970s South Georgia
island genii girls
fans of Eden
living in beach-houses
inside our washed-up

unvaxxed vacuums,
blooming bottles of
spellbinding *Arabian Nights*
book-kameradin
drizzled ever-ebbing
star-studded dreams
in 70-degree sunny
yestery-year blizzards

MARILYN JOHNSTON

Dear Mr. Stafford

It's 3:45am here. I've been following you across
the pages of your books on my writing desk.
I've borrowed your silences, the way they flow
between words, weaving them into my own
pauses, as if these breaths were mine to exhale.

And, sometimes, your poems, like stones
smoothed by time, skip across the surface
of my thoughts like ripples, then expand—
intersecting, as though a conversation
everyone can hear.

In "Ask Me," I've tried to channel you,
inviting the incarcerated youth in my
writing class to pose a searing question—
point a finger at themselves in the mirror,
seek an unerring truth.

So, thank you, William Stafford, for turning
your observations into our own lenses
through which to see the light—
holding your poems up to our eyes,
letting them bathe there.

LIBBY FALK JONES
Alone, Together

For William Stafford

What if we were alone?

I caught up with you
in the vestibule of the college chapel
where you'd read your poems to an audience
way too small, considering it was you.

What if there weren't any stars?

I loved your poem about being alone,
the way it moves through a universe of rocks and light,
finding, finally, a glimmering connection.
I wanted that poem for my utopias class,
this was 1991, I was teaching Berea College first-years
to reach out, to dream.

*What if no one ever found anything outside
this world right here?*

Where could I find that poem? I asked—
and you reached into the top pocket of your blue shirt,
not fancy, something a Kentucky workman might wear,
and tugged out a wad of small pages.
You flicked through them, like a cashier making change,
and pulled out one page.

*We are led outward. We glimpse
company.*

I held your poem in my hand.
Your typewriter was my mother's vintage,
keys slightly askew. With your pen
you'd made small changes
on the page.

*What kind of listening
can follow quietly enough?*

In my hand—your poem.
I thanked you, we smiled,
and all the planets kept turning together.

LISA KAGAN
Alphabet of the Moment

Accept this tether
Balance precariously
Construct small shrines
Drink in oblivion
Enter this narrow tunnel
Find a new space for yourself
Give more than you take
Hug with abandon
Intercept dark thoughts
Jump boldly with your eyes open
Kick back
Love shamelessly
Move mountains
Never dishonor yourself
Open
Press gently into possibility
Quiet consideration offers new insights
Rest more than you rush
Speak up
Touch your life with your whole heart
Unearth your treasures
Vivacious vision
eXplain
You are wild
Zoom forward into the moment

GAYLE KAUNE
At the Zoo

At the zoo I saw a mole rat
in its glass-windowed burrow—
such tiny teeth—and when
it looked at me, two inches away,
and yawned I was no longer
disappointed that the leopard
had slept in the shade camouflaged
by its perfect spots.

At the zoo I watched two camels
wrestle with each other.
Not fighting, but leaning over
and under and taking
the other's foot in its mouth.
"Like a game of twister,"
my grandson remarked and the docent lady
said they were siblings and play constantly.

At the zoo my oxygen supply was running low
so I sat at the entrance and waited
for my family to circle back.
I watched a bouquet of young school children,
dressed in bright shirts (even the boys!),
gathered up by a teacher—
—President's Day and a time for field trips.

At the zoo people observed me:
old lady with cannula up her nose.
I didn't care. I sketched the Palo Verde
and its thin branches, no leaves,
while the midday sun carried memories
of past visits when I breathed
without machine. No matter. My eyes
still worked and the toddler
across the plaza, just learning to walk,
stumbled towards me, arms outstretched,
as if I were his grandma.

SARAH KEENEY
Hobbies

I was in a mood,
so, I went to look for birds
and that did the trick.

ELLEN GIRARDEAU KEMPLER

On the Day of Donald J. Trump's Election as 47th President of the United States: Notice What This Poem is Not Doing

After William Stafford

In Istanbul the sun lifts over the Bosphorus,
glancing off the domes of 3,000 mosques,
naming each one holy with the rising call
to prayer.

Notice what this poem is not doing.

From Taksim Square to Gezi Park
monuments mark leaders of conquest
not protest. *How much of this place
is yours?*

Notice what this poem is not doing.

Every strongman guarding a door
at Istanbul Airport wields a gun.
To use the public Wi-Fi, you must
register your passport number.

Notice what this poem is not doing.

P.M. Erdoğan peers sharply from
large billboards across the city. In
Topkapi Palace gardens, covered
women crouch like black crows
in intensive threat posture.

Notice what this poem has not done.

PAMELA KENLEY-MESCHINO
Narrative Assignment

I've learned to be grateful, she says,
for the father who came first before taking
off on his own adventure, for the mother
she aspired to be like, her best friend,
who found freedom across borders only
to die unexpectedly, leaving her alone
to navigate the world. She's grateful,
she writes, for her work, her studies,
her impending graduation, a journey
toward fearlessness and holding her own.
She's grateful for friends who don't underrate
her story, this one she rarely tells except
for now to a blank screen and me with
assignment questions on the other side.
She'll be a nurse, she says; she already
understands the curative power of empathy,
the distinction of courage and perseverance.
She's not looking for accolades or commiseration,
she wants to be clear. She's grateful for those
who forged a trail toward her destiny, the desperate,
the brave, the love and struggle. All of it.
Her words reach me where I sit, poised to enter
a grade where I should be awarding a medal.

LIZ KINGSLEY
A Haiku

Does constructive criticism really exist?
It's not building me.

SABRINA KIRBY

January 9, 2025

Dante, old friend, I think I understand. What would it be like
now, to know that singing Spheres embrace us, a Primum Mobile,
an Empyrean, where we might, if gifted with your elevation,
see a God right now, and from where that God sees all, infuses
all things with Love, even now, when we feel your same impatience
with so much ignorance, chaos, destruction, all the horsemen loosed
into the world already; our dread, rage, and doubt fueled by real fires
and evil's free reign, enough to plunge a poet, say, into despair,
and drive that poet to bolster faith by yoking art and knowledge
to experience, to make (as poets can, as your Virgil did) a universe
where goodness is not absent but pervasive, yours by the grace
of a whole and complete Trinity: Creator, Redeemer, Holy Spirit
brooding over all? I write "Spirit" and a January robin startles
awake outside my window, bespeaking another vast and complex
pattern. While to the south, snow geese fall from the sky.

CYNTHIA BRIGGS KITTREDGE
Frostbit Bamboo

This is the third winter that freeze
killed the bamboo, the Clumping
Bamboo that towers at the border
of our lot and in the spring
rattles and sings in the breeze.
It's not the nuisance bamboo
that people try to extricate,
but the beautiful bamboo that
was solace around us when
we were confined.
The wrens call from there
but you can't even see them
just their rustle.
The leaves have turned ash
the green drained and dried
and I know what will happen
they'll drop, all of them,
and the stalks will be left
and the gardener will cut them
out at the base and haul them away.
All that bare air round the
windows again this year won't say
"Be patient" or "It's all OK" but
as they fall, untimely loss again,
they whisper, "Horror."

DENISE KREBS
Remember

After Joy Harjo

Remember the warm summer early evening
    on which you were born.
Remember the lights celebrating your birth—
    the sun was shining so brightly
    and the waxing gibbous moon took over
    the celebration a few hours later.
Remember your mama and dada delighting in you, holding you,
    whispering love to you.
Remember I was holding you in my heart for months before
    I got to hold you in my arms.
Remember this morning (though I'm over
    a thousand miles away from you)
    I still and forever will hold you in my heart.
Remember the Love of the universe,
    in you, in all of creation.

MICHAEL LAINOFF
Ode to an Albatross

O you majestic and misunderstood
Master of the sky—
your splendid wingspan propels
across countless leagues,
returning to perch upon
tropical rocky shores, home again
with soulmate and community.

O harmless avian, why
have you been forsaken by
so many earthbound anthros?
You descend from dinosaurs
You descend from the sky
To rest, to feed, to dance
and mate and dance again—

O resilient bird, please
forgive my misassociations,
my unmindful misdemeanors—
I know you're not the emblem of
misfortune—fly on unmolested,
today and forever.

MARTHA LANDMAN
Like Mistletoe

Carefree university days, students laze in the shade on campus lawns—Pretoria University, crown of the town. It's the end of spring and exam-time looms. They chat about their fears, work left undone when too much time was spent on partying, camping and chasing fun. Jacaranda in bloom floods the city. Students cling to the belief, the sure sign that when a flower drops on your head you'll pass the exams. Heads turn to books, cram as much as you can, study day and night. By the end of it, flowers are gone.

>agapanthus blooms
>jacarandas disappeared
>summer in full swing

Years later the world is in disarray. Wars, earthquakes, floods, power hungry men and women disturbing peace. Ovid tells us it's nothing new. I don't agree with him as far as school shootings go, that's twenty-first century. Formal study long gone, I still have the need-to-know—curiosity about life in previous centuries, where did it all start, what was it like then? But most of all, what makes us tick? Why do we do what we do? To still my mind I drive through the Flinders Ranges, soak up the sense of eons-old harmony where rock, soil and air are in unison with plants and wildlife, shallow streams meander through dry land. I hear the elders in the trees, in the breeze, their wisdom unending.

>hills embrace flatlands
>falcons and crows swoop the air
>equilibrium

Restless as a hunted deer, eager as tumbleweed, I travel into unknown territory, find beauty everywhere—mind-blowing art at the Vatican, enormity of the Eiffel Tower, but it is the softness of Devon fields, endlessness of farmlands in northern France that catch my breath. Like mistletoe I can make any place my home if it is countryside. Give me wandering cows and sheep, soaring kites, bike rides through sleepy villages, the gentleness of Sheepwash. An old tortoise, I carry home on my back.

soft breeze combs the plains
ripe fields of corn and barley
sky a blissful blue

CHRISTINA VALENTINE LARSEN
Adulting

Today I give up, give in
I'm not in the mood to adult—at all—ever again
Drastic?
Yes!
Since everyone around me is trying to take that role
I should be able to give it away
I've proved myself
Two husbands
Three daughters
Stepchildren
Two college degrees
A published book
A business or two or three
Hell… a triathlon
Sixty-mile breast cancer walk
Survivor/ thriver

Step back—move aside
You ain't seen nothin' yet

I'm still NOT adulting

M.E. LEE
Confidence

Some
people wear
confidence like
a ball gown, strutting their
stuff, showing off their finest

But me, I
wear a robe
of insecurity
constantly reevaluating, readjusting,
making sure I'm
fully covered

I wish
I could don
a gown whenever
I needed to, but somehow

I always
end up
in my robe,
tying and retying the belt that
threatens
to expose
my many
vulnerabilities

CATHY CULTICE LENTES
Limen

A thin place   edge   end place
smushed against a beginning
a door
raised foot   hand on frame
body leaning   pause
part in part out
      temperature dips
      or rises
air loosens
      or tightens
breath calms
      or heightens
let fate   Trust
find footing
eyes open
      ears open
            mouth tight
or wide in wonder
no going back
      going back
      could turn back
scent of rosemary
            lingering
step again now forward
heels lift
toward light
that might be
could be
could be a
dawn.

DEANNA LERNIHAN

Untitled, in the Garden

The true story is that
a civilization collapsed
and the people wandered
deserts dreaming of a drench
they could hold between the cup
of their palms.

    There was great sadness.

Maybe more sad
is the other true story
of a people who turned their backs
on a land fruiting
with mold, on ideologies
stolen and stored in corrosion-free
polyethylene barrels
marketed for "indoor and outdoor" use
and the people, anyway, had been grafted
on a nationless ancestor

longing to revert
from, say, a self-fertile,
blushing "empire"
to wild Malus *sieversii*—
an apple never to embody
the strangeness of ornamental

or from that fleshy, uniformly red
tomato "celebrity"
to Solanum *pimpinellifolium*
vining deserts and coastlines
unconcerned with its yield
unafraid of having its softness cored
and pulp wind-scattered anywhere
because we are longing

            to become

free of human propagation
feel ourselves strewn
across eroded asphalt
taken in the gut of a bird
hoping one day we'll reach
some storied potential.

KATH LIEFFORT
Antiques Roadshow

In the end, it was all he could watch on TV.
Antiques Roadshow did not remind him
of abandoning his children when
we were all under 10.
How he womanized, his infidelity
the child porn or the molestation.

The show was about a series of individuals
who brought their pieces of art or furniture
from the depths of their attics,
what those individuals hoped had enormous value.
Some were stunned when a piece was worth more
then the amount they earned their entire lives.

I remember when he was about 65 he told me that
he had no sex drive anymore.
I had no interest, no sympathy.
But, *Antiques Roadshow*, intrigued me.
Why this show? Perhaps it was his hope
To have enormous and unexpected value.

ANNA CHRISTINE LINDER-SKACH

Anna Christine Imagines Her Funeral

Inspired by Rosemerry Wahtola Trommer

I want it to be said
I was the kind of woman
who put apples on top of the
garbage cans every Monday,
and one in the mailbox.
I was the kind of woman
that listened. Listened
with the ear of her heart.
I want it to be said
I was the kind of woman
who made a Skippy Extra Crunchy
peanut butter sandwich for a street
dweller, who I looked in the eye
and asked him his name.
I want it to be said
I was the kind of woman
who continually asked the unanswerable questions:
where did I come from? who am I? why am I here?
how should I live? where am I going? what is
the purpose of life? And, the unmentionable, death:
does it have a purpose?
what do you need to know about me before I die?
why is this stuff important?
I want it to be said
I was the kind of woman
that, when I took my last breath,
and my heart took its last beat, and my soul
shed my earthly suit, I smiled with satisfaction.
Job well done. Why? Because we transform each other
in ways we may never know. One of life's mysteries.
I have one final request.
Please use my death as an opportunity
to face your own death.
Go home. Look in the mirror.

Take a deep breath and look into your eyes.
Then ask yourself, is there anyone you need to say,
... I'm sorry... Thank you... I love you...
It could be others, or it could be yourself.
You have been given one life—one unique life.

SUSAN J. LITTLEFIELD
Re-Claiming Warrior Within

Instead of beat the boys; Stand in personal power.
Instead of going one up or one down; Center in perfectly imperfect.
Instead of doing to impress; Take action from stillness.
Instead of girls against boys; Embody fierce feminine and tender masculine.
Instead of catering to the external; Source true heart longing.
Instead of Do, Do, Do; Stop. Sit. Ask.
Instead of blocking love; Feel the dream.
Instead of reaching for phone; Breathe in belonging.
Instead of See me, See me, See me; Witness wild child within.
Instead of I'm too much; Express untamed love.
Instead of raging at society; Heal inner battle and offer peace to the world
Instead of poor me, it's all too much; Reclaim power by asking, "What is mine to do?"
Instead of I'm all alone in this crazy world; Receive spirit's love and Earth's rooted welcoming.

SVETLANA LITVINCHUK
Alive Forever

I steal precious moments here and there
throughout the day while tending to my child
to try to get something,
anything accomplished.

But as she latches onto my breast,
her tired eyes look into mine to ask me,
what could be more important
than watching her sleep,

than listening for her breath,
than this moment we will not have again,
even amid the thousand other moments
just like this one.

And I don't know how to explain
that what I'm doing is so very important.
That by writing this poem I'm trying
to keep from falling so deeply and completely

into this love that I worry
any minute my heart might explode from fullness.
So, I whisper, I'm doing this to keep myself alive
for you forever, as I watch the years drift away.

KRISTINOEL LUDWIG
Morning Haiku

smoke rises on the wind
sunrise in the Eastern sky
I'll spend today's gold

EMILIE LYGREN
Love Letter to the Moon

I feel a tang of hunger each time the moon rises
I want to ingest the edges of her round form.

Light, in a soft ring. In my mind it's fragrant
like white flowers in the night,

like damp Earth, like a perfume
of days stripped to their essence.

Moon, I'll go umber for you,
I'll cover myself in dirt,

I'll wish myself up like a ladder
to press my face against your dust.

No I won't step on you. Nothing
so patriotic or patriarchal.

We'll thunder like horses at midnight,
a meeting of mind and gleam.

I'll dress myself in your glow.
I'll reach you before the sun rises.

M. L. LYONS
Embrace Me, Earthling

We are small of paw,
but large of heart, earthling.
Gather us into your arms.
Embrace us for we are
your true familiars, your private
totems, the spirit creatures who lay
our heads down tenderly on
hearth and earth alike.
We were born to such things.
We warm your winters and
sweeten your lives in summer's blaze.
When you play, we will joy
your every moment in countless
ways and when sorrow leans
upon your shoulder and troubles
your sight and you long for the
tenderness of childhood's days,
we will soundlessly surround you and
with every brush of fur, fin or wing
bare your soul so that the very sight
of us will bring your heart to Heaven.

DORY MAGUIRE

Genealogy

Born from the wind,
running with the wind,
chasing the wind.
We speak ourselves into being.
The stories we tell define us.
We are who we say we are.
We are who we think we are.
We are always moving—
    toward more.
We unleash ourselves on
    the thundering shore.

STACIE MARINELLI
Foxtrot

My parents did the foxtrot,
rhumba, cha-cha, mambo, joined
together in a marriage of movement.
Down the generations, my grandfather
did old fashioned steps with his wife,
forceful ballroom dancing with the man
guiding the woman around the floor.

To dance well one must *need*
to dance, to crave it, to transform
a dancefloor into a farming field,
an art arena, an expanding universe
that can be traversed to an inner voice,
so those who attempt the art
don't just go through the motions,
but sail into the wind.

When my father heard music,
song poured from his mouth,
sound moved his feet, symphonic chords
filled his mind, just as those who
paint/write/sculpt/design/sew
are propelled by an inner impulse,
just as the poem I wrote at age six
has stayed with me as the moment
writing became my unstoppable force.

DOROTHY P. MARSHALL
Untethered

Untethered, I set off in a small boat;
I had no oars, no tiller, and no sail.
I trusted in her sturdiness to float
through ev'ry kind of weather without fail.
I thought back to a story I'd been told
about three Irish monks in days of yore;
they set off in a coracle, quite bold
in their belief that they would reach a shore.
But there was I, without a shore in sight,
adrift upon the ocean of my soul.
I knew I'd have to face the long dark night…
for finding joy and peace exacts a toll.
I chose to trust the journey I was on
and, lo, the starless night gave way to dawn.

CATHERINE LYNN MARTELL
I Am One

At peace,
Who I want
And need to be.
Finally,
A story writing herself.

KAREN MCCASKEY
Awakening

It's cold tonight:
She closes her drapes,
beautiful burgundy shield
keeps away the dark she
no longer needs to see.

An inner darkness
surrounds and holds her,
keeps her safe from
emotional harm.

And when the moon is full,
she wanders alone
bathing in the soothing lunar light,
lets it feed her magic
awaken something deep within,
older than the dark,
older than moonlight.

An ancient spirit, yes,
dragon breathing fire, with
knowledge of all that is mystical—
breathes into her soul
insatiable thirst for freedom so
she shakes the dust off her wings
and flies, in search of a new
tomorrow.

JAY MCCOY
Aftercare

It can become putrid if left
too long in summer heat, naked
on the porch or scattered, dry
between rows of sweet corn.

It will fare no better perched
in a poplar, vine-strangled
among honeysuckle, or impaled
in warning on blackberry thorns.

It may begin to rot with even a kiss
of humidity common in a Kentucky June.
To handle poetry properly, please listen
to ancestors—their weathered hands

spotted with wisdom earned toiling
troubles in depleted, parched soil.

TOD MCCOY

Wellness Check

For BJM, 1936-2025

Did you arrive safely?
Did the clouds slow you down?
Did you meet anyone along the way? Was it far?
Was there a line to get in? Were there gates?
Did you have to recite scripture before entering?
Did you see all the people you ever knew?
Did they cheer when you got there,
or did they fall to their knees weeping?
Are grandma and grandpa happy to see you? Your brother?
Did you see dad? Did you wish him
a happy birthday? Today's his birthday.
Will you spend eternity with him, or with Pete?
Good ol' Pete. You had fun with him.
I bet he's happy to see you.
Did you introduce him to grandpa?
You always said Pete reminded you of your dad.
Did your friends smile and hug you?
Did your enemies boo you?
But you didn't have enemies.
You never embraced the dark side
of human life the way I did.
Did they hand you a gown, a harp, a halo?
Was there golden light and ambrosia to drink?
Did you meet Jesus? What's he like?
Did he smell of sandalwood or like a sweaty hobo?
Did he really say all of those things,
or did people put words in his mouth?
Is it everything you expected?
Are you happy?
Will we see each other again?
Is Heaven only for the Christians?
Were you right all along?

MEGAN MCDONALD
Listen to Poets

read
the news
feel the color of
red flame words
listen to winds of years
of neglect
there are no blue rain showers
glistening in the
power of endless
Santa Ana winds
firefighter's water
is the only source
of mud
understand
the truth of our
failures
light is lost to smoke

WENDY MCVICKER
Half a Poem

Some days, only half
a poem appears,
a cracked rock gleaming

in the dirt. The story
falls away, the rock
remains. Did a cow

step on it, coming back
from pasture, her weight
swaying, her thoughts

on the warm barn
and the sweet breath
of her sisters?

This rock, carried in
from the path, is only
a small part of the story.

It rests on my desk, cradles
a tiny Buddha. Sometimes
the story opens, sometimes

the wind passes through,
rock and Buddha unmoved.

PAIGE MENGEL
Letting Go

He is letting go
Bit by small bit
His body is worn,
He's tired of it.
He's been a cop,
And fisher of men,
He's been a butcher,
He's been a friend.

He's watched friends
And family leave,
But faith is strong
He still believes.
Is it his time?
Only God can say.
She can just watch
As he fades away.

ABBY MEYSENBURG
The Robin and the Worm

Under foretelling skies of gray,
My feet traverse the trails made of concrete.
A puddle reaches up and goes through
The fabric of my shoe and to my sock.
Traversing on the down slope,
My eyes spot a breast of light orange,
An eye pointed towards me, and a beak with a worm.
The dangling worm is swinging back and forth.
Wings come out lifting the robin into the air
Before landing on concrete.
The worm drops; I pause.
The robin takes off again
Without the wriggling worm.
My eyes glanced at it on the concrete
As it wiggles and wiggles,
But one half doesn't move,
A foretelling of its future.

KIMBERLY A. MILLER
Miracle in a Cup

A cluster of a day
Begins with no coffee.
Carting yourself off to the gym
Demanding of yourself to stick to a routine
Expecting yourself to snap out of it and
Find some balance.
Giving yourself permission to be
Half-hearted in your workout,
Inertia spurs you to continue while thoughts
Jumble in your head like a
Knot that won't untangle, which
Limits your ability to be fully present
Making intelligent thought a chore.
No wonder you stop for coffee;
Operation rescue the day commences.
Perhaps this is a vain hope, a
Quixotic belief that
Rationality will reenter your head by
Sipping on a simple cup of
Terrible mass-produced coffee, but
Under the circumstances you had
Very little choice as
Weary, the cup with the
Xiphoid stirrer, has become
Your hope that your head will get in the
Zone and function normally.

PAULA BAUGHMAN MILLER
Night Warrior

In the deep
hours of the night,
after the onset
of her dementia,
my tiny mother
would wake, confused,
yet deftly navigate
the darkness
from her room,
down the hallway
to my room,
lean her face
into mine,
and say my name,
tentatively,
questioningly...

The battle
against
Alzheimers'
fierce grip
of confusion
and fear
was most palpable
when the shadows
of the evening
enveloped her
inner and outer world.

I miss her
soft-shoe shuffling
ninja powers
of silent tenacity
and stealth
love.

CLAYTON MOON
Amber Ember

 Amber Ember
Burn so tender,
  Shaded-spurn,
For November.

 I gaze upon your flicker,
    Smokey Oak, pumpkin wicker.
Coffee stout,
      bitten-bitter.

Sweet gum embers I stoke,
  Inhaling…
        persimmon tokes,
With
Circling crisps
     of sycamore smoke.

My life-long dream,
  Sizzle in-between,
Crackles of Ember's beams.

Burning Cedar wood,
 I'd go back, if I could,
Shine like I should… .

  But,
    The
     Ember holds me here,
Faced with burning fears,
 So,
   I shed my ashful tears.

In forgotten forests of peace,
  My fire burns as you cease,
With the final embers you release.

Lay pecan split on flames,
  Thankful for the fire I tamed,
But,
  My Ember is unusually,
           the same.

Every night, soft moon,
  Flourishing midnight tunes,
Gurgling creeks with whispering loons.

Smoke dances West,
  Anticipating what is next,
Ember reflects a cardinal's breast.

 Signaling my desire,
   Enraging my soul's fire,
Flames, flame higher!

 My path intertwined,
   With the
    Blackness of a walnut's rhine,
Knotted in a sculppernong divine.

Pines invite morning light,
  Amber sky, silences the night,
Ember rays, Ember sight.

Maple leaves sway,
As the Ember fades,
    my
  Mindless journey stays.

Intrigued by orange-red,
  Matching scarlet sheds,
Smoldering life from the dead.

I glow as well,
  Ember aging my tale,
Before igniting my farewell.

While,

My thoughts empty to ashes,
   Of my life's daring dashes,
Fading to faithful flashes.

Just moments, burning,
   In my whirlwind turning,
Amber memories yearning.

To be
Relived, and embraced,
   Without fear I faced,
Ember, remain in place.

Your warmth in cold,
   As my face grays old,
Every fire, a tale to be told.

Amber Ember
   I always remember,
Reflecting shades of November.

   —Boxer

MISHA MOON

Let Me Love This Horrible World

I became an old woman, always mother
and never virgin or whore. I hid my
pretty face in the shame of a beard

for too many decades, defined myself
worthy of hate. Let me love this body,
soft and bristly sometimes, curved by

science and magick. Let me love this
horrible world, push against men who
see me as sex or guilt, against women

who see me as an enemy, punch down
to easy ways to win, not up towards
structures built on girders of binaries.

I hoped to find more women like me,
hoped genitals lost their power over
who gets to live like themselves now.

Let me love this horrible world, wake
without friends feeling a pull towards
razors when others perceive us. Let me

love this horrible world, sun dressed,
clocked by mystery, the last years left
guffawing my way to heaven right here.

KATE MCCARROLL MOORE
Ode to My Old Hands

There was a time
when, without thinking,
I could pour coffee from the pot,
tie my shoes, open a jar, fasten a chain
around my neck. I whistled without thinking
while putting the baby in her car seat,
pulling an errant weed, straining the pasta,
filling the bird feeders, walking the dog.
My fingers, then, were diamond ringed, polished and
smooth. They danced hello and goodbye at the end
of crisply ironed sleeves. Two graceful birds fluttering
in the summer breeze. Embracing present tense.
Happily oblivious to what the future could hold.

CHANDRA TYLER MOUNTAIN
You'll Hear Music

If you listen closely—

you'll hear the music in the quiet humming,
pulses and surges of electricity,
moving through us
with light and energy.

If you listen closely—

you'll hear the music in the wind
whistling softly, making its way through,
carrying seeds of hope
for a tomorrow that will surely come.

If you listen closely—
you'll hear the music in the stately elms and oaks
planning for a winter
of full exposure:
cold days, stark nights.

If you listen closely—

you'll hear the music in the private chirps
of the feathered ones who remain
to brave the winter and feast on songs of insects
buried deep in the cold, hard earth.

If you listen closely—

you'll hear the music in the laughter of children
frolicking in the last remaining days of sun
before the arctic breeze pushes us behind closed doors
to seek other sources of warmth.

If you listen closely—

you'll hear the music in the beating of your own heart
in tune with blessing and grief,
singing back to you:
all is well; all is well.

CHARLY MULLAN
25 Stars!

I had fallen for your style,
Romance, and
Pure love, but
Have held off from your long stories.

I couldn't believe you could hold
My wishful heart in
The spread of your writing.
Tangle me in your words.

Delight my imagination with
Constant reminders of
What it takes to be a man
While holding me in the beat of
Your erotic voice
That loving poetic pulse.

I can only say, now,
That empty hole I've felt deep in my longing,
Has been quenched with orgasmic belief in
Possibilities,
Creative visualizations, and
Tears of joy.

Yes, there can be more than
The perfect
"One-night story… "

NANLEAH
Summer Stars

Plunge into your dusky roots,
rise with the forget me nots.

They are not that different
from the stars, their azure universe

organized from the inside out,
with golden points of light

at their center where bees
thrum then dance

so others may sip stars.

BONNIE NARADZAY

Cloud of Unknowing

> *"All I do is eat, sleep, drink, and be negligent."*
> John of Dalyatha, monk and mystic (690–780)

Just how did Paul arrange his days?
All those Epistles must have taken time.
Distraction was not possible for him.
One monk moved into a pharaoh's tomb
to get away from it all. But in the shards
he left behind, it seems he was busy
arranging deliveries of spices (cardamom)
or asking his sister for clothes and food,
although fasting is said to focus the mind.
Sleeping can keep one from praying
unceasingly so was often discouraged,
but why fight a losing battle? No rest
for the weary, my mother used to say,
though she stayed in bed later each day,
practicing negligence, dreaming away.
Simeon of Stylites lived on top of a pillar
for over 35 years near Aleppo, which must
have been hard to do. What could he do
but pray and stare at the sun up there?
Why do minds wander during prayer?
John of Dalyatha lived in a monastery
on the same mountain where Noah's ark
was found, which could have sparked
his concentration in a profound way.
I went to Madonna House downtown
to stay overnight in their Poustinia
space and promptly fell asleep,
feeling not negligent, but released.
Prayer can lead to a meditative state—
a cloud of unknowing, a mystical place.

JOSEPH NEELY
Forsythe Junior High

Dream on, little boy

My wife and I attended the same school
for one year, in 1967,
though she was two years older
and we didn't know each other,
or so she claims.

But there must have been a moment
we passed each other in the hallway
when some spark passed between us,
and nagged at us both, inexplicably,
for the rest of the day.

I'm convinced, in fact,
she had a crush on me—
or at least found me intriguing—
though she didn't know my name
or my favorite Beatles song
and just the other day,
when I suggested this to her,
she laughed and said, "Ninth grade girls
didn't care about seventh grade boys."

But still, I think she liked me,
even if she didn't know it then
and won't admit it now.

WILL NIXON
Everything

I changed my name to Whatever
& forwarded all emails to the President
in charge of our national insanity, while I taught
David Bowie to ride elephants, giddy-up, giddy-up.

I recorded my heartbeat for a pirate DJ,
not the emperor monopolizing the moon for immortality.
I woke up to the apocalypse & went out for breakfast,
salsa & eggs & gold in my cigarettes.

I improved my cursing by drinking vinegar
Kombucha & watching *Mad Max* at 1.25 speed.
I skipped the invitation to join the Society of the Brave
& lie on a bed of nails till closing time.

I died shortly before dawn, but what a year.
I'm not telling anyone except a few billionaires.
I was also reborn shortly before dusk. Like I said,
I was everything & its opposite. At least in Paris.

NAOMI SHIHAB NYE

Marfa

A departed boy now owns all his ages at once.
He is 5, 10, 15. I feel him in the joyous years,
drawing graphs at poetry readings,
small arrows pointing to
"really boring" or "slightly better"
selections.

Now, at 3am. I jolt awake.
Here come the "really worst" thoughts.
We can't believe he'll never be
hopping into the car again,
dragging his golf clubs to Fort Worth,
shooting his famous three pointer ball
from the corner of the yard.

When morning comes,
who wants to rise?
My brain whirls, spins in its socket.
Not ready for coffee, unable to comfort itself.
I feel my father wailing for the children of Gaza
who never hurt anyone in their lives. Wailing for
his grandson, who hugged a chicken and always
made him laugh. In the stars,
the dark, a gentle man sobs for the universe.
Maybe they're all together now, I wish.
There is nothing good to tell him.

Why, if we were so happy in Marfa,
have I never gone back in 20 years?

JENNY OLSON
Silhouettes at Night

no bare trees in winter
leafless and stark
such beauty

no, the silhouettes
are in my mind
seared there
night friends
standing against a wall
on that corner
or on that corner
in a doorway
or walking
all selling
not only some fantasy
but our souls

silhouettes of the past
of a time long gone
imposed on the current world
as etchings on my eyes

some names forgotten
but not their faces
do they remember me too?

some stories we told each other
the important ones we didn't
couldn't show weakness
on streets that would eat us alive

secrets tucked so deep inside
mine took decades
to start coming out
box would open; slam it shut fast

silhouettes at night
black ghosts of another era
helped each other to a certain point
stabbed each other in the back just as easily
but we were beautiful
        we were strong
                and i got out
                        many didn't

watch the leaning ones start to move
heading away from the track
the walking ones keep on walking
back to where we went
before the sun rose

so many years later
i hear what i told myself then
girl, look at you, way too thin
circles under your eyes
makeup doesn't conceal
and you call this taking your life back?
that voice still lingers today
though that woman's been
gone for many years

that woman standing in a shop doorway
still lives in my heart
she's the powerful part of me
and i love her dearly
her name was Jenny
she's the part that writes
my words/my truth/my magic
a silhouette from another age
who still lives

CAROL CLEMENTE O'MALLEY
Reflections

From each September to the next
Our lives are like the sea
Forever rolling with reflections
Of what is and what could be

Sparkling water reflects the days gone by
Crystals of sand
The sun in my eye
Bathers and swimmers
Alone in the crowd
Lovers and Dreamers
Thinking out loud

The memories of winter
The flowers of spring
Sail in my dreams
on a nightingale's wings

Life was so simple
The air was so clear
In the days of yesteryear
We sailed through our sorrow
With 'there's always tomorrow'

As a faraway song
Fills a moment in time
A lonely child listens and beckons
Please place your hand in mine

By the shore on a blanket
Oh the reflections we will see
Our yesterdays and tomorrows
Sailing on waves of immortality.

HEATHER ONEAL
Finding Beauty

Almost eight years of wondering and wandering
In depths of despair and hopefulness
In searching and not knowing.
Almost eight years of reaching for answers
In curiosity and broadening awareness
In righteous anger and defeat.
Almost eight years of stepping into newness
In between balance and the cliff edge
In uncertainty and sharpened wisdom.
Almost eight years of finding myself
In the deepening trust and resilience
In the expansive shifts of tidal sands.
Almost eight years of leaning in and learning
In the energetic space of wholeness and loss
In the wilderness coming together in beauty.

DIANE O'NEILL
What Is the Meaning?

Is life a story penned by a Creator,
plot points to test us
the way we writers challenge characters?
      I tend to look at my life as a story
bad stuff—childhood trauma, my own sins—
leading to good stuff
      but is that just my manipulation
because I like happy endings?
      Is there a heaven
a smiling God waiting to greet us
(or maybe Saint Peter, his main guy)
and do we meet loved ones
and even, by some multi-colored bridge, our pets?
      That would be bliss—for isn't a real friend
someone you can do the boringest thing with
say, go to the laundromat, and you're
having a great time regardless—so
endless eternity days would work.
      Will we look down on loved ones
still here? Jacqueline Woodson
in her YA novel imagines the dead always with us…
      Or is life merely random atoms and cells
playing havoc, delighting in randomness?
      I know I feel like a world
and I know you do, too—we're all worlds
jostling against each other.
      If those who endured painful existences
are snuffed out like candles, how can there be meaning?
      And yet people fall in love
babies are born, someone donates a kidney
to a passing stranger—
      Could love,
not just romantic Romeo and Juliet passion
but friendship, plain ol' love to fellow humans
be a cord, giving us something to hold on to
as we search for life's purpose
      and could that be the meaning?

KATE O'NEILL
Before You Leave Joyce Country

Go collect light reveries—gather a fistful
of whisps shapeshifting into linen skies
as water ruffles like age-old druid birds
slightly before sunrise.

Bring back May bush honey
from Maam where bleating lambs
jerk milk and a spare ineffable
foots-it across lemony wood sorrel.

Gather a flint of quartz from the steep
pitch of fields between the Maumturks
and the gorse-covered yellow Bens, then braid me
an instance of tender rushes plaited into a Brigid's cross.

Make your way to Finny and gather me a drop spindle
of fleece from the blackface sheep of the hill,
as you glimpse a pygmy goat and her kid
grazing purple-blue elderberries.

And, if you witness the wooden anvil of a rowboat
drifting the shores of Lough Nafooey,
trailing ripples like contours on a low-lying
map, garner me those curves.

Climb up the Pass of Birds to the edge
of that wind-swept Celtic well,
where four Dara hum and sway—
droning in unison to a subtle pulse.

Hail them quite kindly—
then bring me that pulse.

ASHER PACKMAN
The Forge of Being

The hammer and the anvil,
the molten river of hardening iron,
the ache in the arm of the smithy,
and the silence between strikes.

To be a man is to carry the stone,
not to conquer it but to know its shape,
the cold bite of its truth
and the warmth of its endurance.

To be a man is to kneel
in the dirt beneath you,
knowing it will one day claim you.

It is to hear the whisper of ancestors
echoing in your marrow.

To be a man is to fall in love
with the questions,
while the Trickster's grin mocks
your need for answers.

It is to hold the flame of your own longing.

To be a man is to walk the labyrinth
and meet yourself in the centre,
offering the only thing worth owning:
a heart that dares remain open.

DONNA M. PADGETT
"Will She Get Over It?" "She Will Never Get Over It!"

Her heart was ripped out, throbbing,
And snapped back in, quivering frantically.
The air was sucked out of her lungs
And difficultly flows in and out again.
She took a gut-punch to her stomach,
Which still aches and rebels.
Tears streamed out her eyes, drying
Bloodshot, dull orbs, deep in sockets.
Her flesh has hollowed out, too,
Leaving her a living skeleton.
Sleep does not come, except in fits and starts,
With snatched dreams of joy or sorrow.
Sometimes it's hard to think
And she curls up, covered, to molt,
But never metamorphoses.
She's always a ragtag remnant,
Sleep-walking through life
In search of what she cannot find,
What she lost, and her former self.

STEVE PAUL
The Columbines Grow

To fix the garden hose takes three tools—screwdriver,
shears, blade—and hands of course and fingers
to finesse the pieces and put them back together,
making the hose leak-free again, or mostly, as
columbine, pink and pale pale violet and purple,
beckons in a way I hadn't seen for years
in the garden—the beds with small Japanese maple,
a hunched-over Harry Lauder, so close to the ground
as if in prayer, emergent plants and veteran hosta,
ground cover not quite covering but aiming to
get the job done. The air is clean and crisp under
the big ginkgo and despite the sorry state of the world,
all might well be well in this precinct of remove
and of tender mercies in a moment
of soft showering care.

JANE PEARSON
So Much Killing

"Our hands are tied", a friend said.
Tied with what, by whom
and aren't we tied to each other?

The water fountain in my yard
spills over and over,
up and over.

Pools of grief invite
the weight of sadness
of centuries to drop and float here.

Under the pools, the Earth braves
us humans, with arms wide open,
and heart big enough.

Some of what I release ceases
to be mine to carry.
I give it to my ancestors,
whose dreams shaped me,
who delighted in my breathing.

With fresh water in hand I settle into a chair.
Pine siskins come, drink
and sit by the fountain.

SARAH JOSEPHINE PENNINGTON
(An American Sentence, In a Private Room on the Med Surg Floor, 2021)

I'd let Ronald McDonald amputate at Play World to end this pain.

CHARLES A. PERRONE

Overture to a Dramatic Monologue

Upon the advice of counsel and counselors alike
I have decided to accept the ad hoc plea bargain
in order to avoid an unartistic harsher sentence:
I do agree to remain here for one year and a day
and to deliver a daily poem or like lyrical instance
to the handlers whose insistence will be so pivotal
if I am to undertake this task with cleaner success
marked by prompt completions between midnights.
For now, I bid you farewell, a domani, hasta mañana,
adieu until the morrow makes it merry way to me.

SHANNON PERRY

Kinship of Douglas Firs

Far above my reach, in clusters of green starbursts
Radiates a haloed crown, a coronet of Douglas Firs
Catching sun sparkles, encircling my head.
A royal grouping of stately trees together
Intermixed with Ponderosa Pine,
I feel my soul rise within this entity.

Each trunk solitary, yet part of one entity
Lifts me skyward on a breeze of starbursts.
The loam rich with past lives under the pine.
In this incarnation, I've grown out of the soil like the Douglas Firs.
The forest sustained me when most kin failed altogether.
Except for my siblings and the woodland at the beachhead.

During darkness out of time, I stumbled ahead
Searching for a guiding entity
When I forgot the ground beneath held me together.
Out of onyx loneliness, bright starbursts
Sharpened my vision and I sit within the Douglas Firs,
Resting again, safe against the sister pines.

When in my youth I left city bound, I did pine,
Never a safe place nor comfort to rest my head.
Wide avenues lined with oak and maple, no Douglas Firs
Though surrounded by many, no kinship in these entities.
Still, at night past those city lights, I glimpsed starbursts
And thus began a trek toward the stand of siblings together

I took a few wrong turns but never a dead end altogether.
The boulders of my errors lay between me and the pines.
Sometimes I fell and spinning, saw starbursts
But they didn't lead, just swirled like wine above my head.
In and out of my blurring, I caught glimpses of an entity
Sure, strong, and sturdy as my Douglas Firs.

Hiking pole in hand I continue my pilgrimage to Douglas Firs.
Full circle I arrive, a lifetime apart and together
Joy-filled, again encircled by fragrant entities
Warmed by sun's rays filtering through the pine
Peace fills my heart, from my toes to my head.
Held aloft from tree to tree by a strand of starbursts.

Thriving, expansive, a carpet of Douglas Firs
My family's embrace, our core together
We are but one entity.

CRISSY ANDERSON PETERS
A Prayer for Lent

Let me surrender
That which does not fulfill love—
Does not anchor strength;
Let me surrender
That which harbors resentment—
Does not strengthen love;
Let me surrender
All that is not genuine—
May I be washed clean.
Each day is a gift;
Let me treat it as such,
In sweet surrender.

MARY LOUISE PETERS
Some Questions

Some questions are canvas sneakers, bunion-holes, frayed shoestrings, worn since forever.

Steel-toed kickers, kitten heel slippers—questions are shoes.

Tread lightly-threadbare questions between pairs walk the years.

Tight-lipped, zipped knee high boots have something to hide. Jaded, festooned cowboy boots have an image to uphold. Some questions limp, some are tough leather.

Shoes lined with cardboard,

souls worn thin are questions that get no answers.

Some questions are hikers worn to the mountain top. Some questions sit crossed-legged.

Sandals or barefooted some questions are humble, exposed; some questions stand right there with you without saying a word. Some questions are patient, some are kind, some do not envy or boast.

JENNIFER PRATT-WALTER

Antlers

i love you
like a caribou
loves her antlers

all the more
because someday
the bones unlock,
giving themselves
to the grateful earth

i love you
like the earth
takes back her antlers
and eventually
her inert body,

life's circular alchemy
written by one who
cannot be
named

VANESSA PROCTOR
Library

The electric doors
of the library slide
open to quietude
at the beginning
of this ordinary day.

All's in order,
every book
in its place,
librarians positioned
behind their desks.

Words and ideas
are neatly stacked,
vibrating within their
soft-stitched enclosures,
waiting for the curious

to come, unleash them,
watch them burst
from their paper beds,
shining and resonant,
into the world.

QUIGLEY PROVOST-LANDRUM
On Seeing Krapp's Last Tape

(with apologies to Samuel Beckett)

First he
eats a banana
as if he
likes it as
if it is
good he hears
the tape words
puzzled he
does not
drink his shadow
drinks
the moment
he hears his
thirty-nine-year-old
voice moments
his hand remembers
he does not
drink his shadow
drinks twice three
times remember
his shadow stays
with the drink
the moment
the loss
maybe he was right
the spool
of what
he was who
earth empty
then the light
it vanishes vanishes
done.

MELISSA RANKIN
Meditation Run

In the early morning hours,
When everyone is sleeping,
My meditation feet take me
To the paved city streets.

A mantra rhythm on the concrete,
The mist of the breaking sun,
The drumming, hummed foot pounding,
Has become an exerted run.

Carried away by the journey,
Deep into thought, I go.
Searching for endless answers,
Looking for what I need to know.

My body is covered with sweat,
At the end of exertion,
The steps taken of inner growth,
Guides me to my destination.

CINDY REDMAN
Like Water

I am like water
flowing through this life;
sometimes calm, persistent;
sometimes turbulent, messy.
Always mirroring the sun
and the moon and the stars
in the many reflections of me.

AMY LE ANN RICHARDSON
We're All Pulled

The Carolina wren calling out won't hush.
She's determined to find a partner
before the coming storm to shelter with,

to build a nest by this blooming
hen-bit and perky bedstraw,
maybe in the tree with the tire swing.

Frogs call and the creek flow is constant,
punctuated by the wren's urgency.
I walk down the driveway, leaving

the warmth of my concrete porch to feel
this gritty gravel against my feet and
bug bites all over my ankles.

I can smell grass and dirt on the coming rain
and dream about the ramps and morels
waiting for me when it passes, as fresh and

delicious as walking out here to see
hillsides covered in green.

CATHY RIGG
Winter Laid Wide

Winter laid wide across the mountains, the flat light
gray and dimensionless as the cold mist
stirred, then settled, then stirred again.

The morning offered little. No sun, no vast sky,
no view to a day made of anything at all
but this dreary season

and bed

and blankets.

KACI RIGNEY
Full Cart

In grocery aisles of my life,
Like butter spread too thin,
I shop around the end caps,
While putting items in.

Items, right and wrong for me;
My full cart weighs me down.
I grunt and groan, push and prod,
The wheels squeak, won't turn 'round.

Round two: throw in this and that,
Which robs me of my time.
Think I can add one more thing,
Which overwhelms my mind.

All day, I shop for items.
Why can't I just say no—
Leave ideas on the shelf?
My friend, I just don't know.

RICHARD ROBBINS
The Wake

I've been going through the slides, flotsam
of Christmases, birthdays, jetsam of
days on the lake, roses in Vancouver,
milk truck my uncle drove. The two dogs.

Eighty slides per tray. Three dozen trays.
No projector that works. I hold each
to light, digitize a few. I'm like this
until I need to stop, breathe again.

We've aged well. The sky has disappeared
but not our colors, especially
under the Chinese elm or anywhere
indoors. The things we kept from weather

dodged the fade: plate of standing rib roast,
Yorkshire pudding, the color of scotch.
My grandfather's bridgework. My mother's laugh.
When I wish for more, it's more faces:

More Uncle Emory leashed to his
oxygen. More cousins in a pile.
More faces with their eyes closed, more noses
picked, more faces with their tongues stuck out.

I'm dusting us all off for the next
50 years of eyes, the new versions
of TIFF. It doesn't matter really I'm
all dust myself, splendid wreckage bobbing

in the wake, passengers slung over
aft rails, some waving, a shearwater
dipping nearby, until other matters
call and the ship sails calmly on.

SHEILA DC ROBERTSON
Blankets of Cold

Like frost on quilted fields
Moonlight spreads my bed
And in the throat of the night
I sense your breathing

Turning to touch
What is no longer
My breath ends
In a low plaintive moan

Again and again
You set out on the hunt
Tramp over the pasture
In boot-squeak snow

Cross over the fence
The crack of a shot
Struggle in the creek
The red splashed ice

Tonight   you hunt west of Orion
With no promises
For empty bellies
Or shattered hearts

I shift into the cold depression
Left by years of your body
Cupping close to mine
Search to fill the emptiness

In dreams I welcome you
Home from the hunt
Cry out as you pass by our bed
Anguished and alone

ZOÉ Y. ROBLES
Flamma Vestalis

We pray for the fire we lost the moment we turned
    away from the familiar horizon. The beating open-hearted
        flame that habitually connects us to the city's past is now spent.

As the night turns, as the dawn rings in quiet light,
    out of the darkness they come. This is no surprise,
        we have called them out with our altars, our dancing.

Who will refuse the offering of bread?
    Who will refuse our evening of story and song?
        Out of the darkness they come as we celebrate the touching of worlds.

What we ask for is guidance, a bread crumb found
    on the road to know we are on the right path, away
        from the anger that makes us open and close our fists at all hours.

We ask for a sign, a murmuration of birds to blanket us in peace
    or make us flee from the incoming violence. We are at a loss at their silence.
        Their hands hover over the remaining cinders as if warming themselves.

We fear it's late now; harsh daylight will erase them from view.
    So, what else can we do other than begin to despair at this hour?
        Then each of them puts an open hand over our clean white tunics.

Over each of our hearts blossoms a quivering tongue of fire
    that is for us to guard and protect without rest or carelessness.
        Each of us turned into lanterns, the path itself an altar to the future.

ADRIANA ROCHA
Bird of Words

Flying among kites,
my poems are born,
Words are food
When seeking substance.

I am a bird of the skies,
My writings
Are memories
Of my flights.

Sunrises and words,
Clouds and poems,
Breezes and songs
Gently caress my feathers and thoughts.

JOE ROCHE
The Sweet, Sweet Spot

Big fat ugly puppet show
turning over and over
like a carcass on a wheel
like a gazelle pulled to the bottom of a pond in an alligator's jaws

that is the scene
that is where the pressure lies
that is the sweet, sweet spot
the erogenous zone
that is what everyone hoots at
and waves flares around
like howler monkeys

money and lambos
and car-grill sized sunglasses
and gucci and dolce and gabana
men with purses they spent six figures on
and cocaine and Cristal
and crypto
and yachts and camgirl porn

dance dance dance dance
and grind some poor mother's memories under your feet.

You can feel it as soon as you wake up:
even the flowers want us dead.

TAMARAH ROCKWOOD
Metamorphosis

For Ovid

As readily as the moon eclipsed the sun;
As smoothly as Io slipped on her heifer skins;
As Daphne raised her arms into laureled branches;
So, did Echo unname herself.

From an autumnal leaf to soil;
A stump abandoned to burrow;
A sunken pit to pond;
A fallow field to flower;

Due to
As to
Unto
Onto
Into

SHELLY RODRIGUE
Wheelbarrow

after William Carlos Williams

so tired
of being

the wheel
barrow

I'd rather
be chickens

peck-
-ing

at drops
of rain

BRIAN ROHR

Once, a Crow Broke Free

Arms raised up to the sky,
birds of all kinds,
crows, robins, finches, doves
circling overhead,
dancing wild to the rhythm of the wind.

One crow broke free from the dissonance
landed before me with curious eyes.
I lowered my arms, looking back
with my own curiosity.

Slowly I placed one hand in my pocket,
drew out a hazelnut,
tossing it about a foot to its left.

Within a beat, the crow snatched it up,
flew west,
away from the flock above.
I walked home,
                              alone,
also westward,
through the empty streets.

It was only later,
upon seeing the hazel branch
outside my front door
that I finally, finally understood.

JENNIFER ROOD
Love Letter

Even if I were to lose my map
I could not lose my way:
I do not know what draws me to you
but it is strong and deep, and
I must return to you
again and again
like a stone tossed into the air
to the earth of your body
where I lie, content,
pressed close and resting,
my heaviness settling
against your bedrock
and as close as I can bring myself
to the bones of you

MICHAEL RUNNING

Rocks of Solitude

This is where they left what remains
along the old trail
behind the blue door
above an unmistakable canyon
where deep amber waters
return naturally to the sea
it is here they gather
in memory
in grief

leafless trees beech and chestnut
preside next to the worn path
with its stone walls
markers of history and forgotten things
higher in the canyon solitary boulders
once fiery now cooled
mold the waters into hushed pools
to rest
to mingle

it is here they gather
to remember and grieve
sharing words of story
in the dim winter light
they scatter the ashes of
this once man
father brother uncle friend
given back to the lands and waters
he loved

fulfilling his final wish
to remain
here

JUNE CRAWFORD SANDERS
Mom's Word Salad

Listen at the back door,
the ring-ships going up the hill—
aren't they pretty?

If they get around to rain
or anything at all
it can be good.

The sugar-feathers
are getting the future,
aren't they?

I'm opening mail
for the Flying Dutchman.

LESLAYANN SCHECTERSON
Red Dirt Ditty

Rusty red southwest mesas
Sculptured places, stone towers
Force of millennial winds
Craft temples for sacred hours.

Ubiquitous Utah sand
Colorful brand of this state
Unrelenting winds cast dust
Everywhere at rapid rate.

Red rust dirt makes thick clay mud
The crud caked on my hiking boots
Flakes to nanoparticles
Now atop my northwest roots.

Utah sand dusts my home floors
Knobs on doors, pebbles on decks
I brush and sweep this fine mess
Everywhere there's still more flecks!

LISA SHAHON
Thursday Morning, 7:20am

Your rhythmic breath
In the darkness beside me
Anchors my world.

RON SHAPIRO
Ode to Tofu

With a name almost like some haiku poet
From before the dawn of modern times,
This white block of tofu floating in water
Solid but not solid for when pressed
The liquid drips down onto the countertop.
Like a brick used to build the pyramids
Or the walls of a house,
Its sturdy shape rests on the cutting board.
Effortlessly the knife blade slips through
The firmness, each slice identical.
Unable to stand on its own now,
The tofu tips over into a swoon
Awaiting whatever
Dish it will find itself in.
Lifted gently now into the pan
Simmering with oil and spices,
The tofu opens its heart to
Assume the flavor desired by a chef.

Sizzle
Sizzle
Sizzle

Like a quick-change artist,
The whiteness
Suddenly browned
At the corners now
Turned over and then
Over again until what
Was once tasteless
And bland evolves into
Perhaps the finest
Crunchy taste ever
Placed in your mouth.

Wonderful tofu!
From an empty snowy
Field transforming
Into a blossoming field
Of flavorful joy!

ERIN T. SIM
Promises

You don't have to make promises
even to yourself.
Promises are as temporary as the weather,
even among the best promise-makers.
Our world is not designed for permanence.
Weather shifts, skies cloudy or blindingly bright
in the twist of a minute.
Frigid air penning you indoors,
frost talking to you on the window glass;
or hot, steamy air pinning you to a porch chair.
One day it's one thing.
The next day, another.
One day your heart clenches with love,
the next it clenches with fear.
They feel the same,
but the landscape is different,
the characters re-cast.
And some days
the heart sits silent in your body,
beating, pumping out of habit,
a promise it made before your birth
which may or may not be kept.
You wonder about the promises
you made to yourself, or another,
or to the unknown force you suspect
scripts the universe, down to the details
of your hand pressing against the frosted glass,
melting the conversation between you
and the frozen water,
just so you can feel,
just so you can feel again
just so you can bring back the clench,
the love your heart felt
on the sun-spattered porch
receiving an icy glass of lemonade
from a hand you promised to love
forever.

MARGARET SIMON
Live Oak Pantoum

Light from the east illuminates leaves
spotting the live oak tree with shadows.
He asks me to stop and look again
as I rush through the sunrise.

Spotting the live oak tree with shadows
I can only describe this feeling by singing
as I rush through the sunrise.
Listen to the melody.

I can only describe this feeling by singing
where roots gather in harmony.
Listen to the melody
of rope swings waiting.

Where roots gather in harmony,
he asks me to stop and look again.
There rope swings are waiting
and light from the east illuminates leaves.

ANDY SMITH

Small Wall

Dedicated to Marilyn who died on the final day of the Stafford Challenge

Let's extend this small wall, she said
And create a flat spot on the slope
For this ancient rock with a fossil in its face
To sit.

Help me if you would,
Pull a basket out of stone and soil
For these flowers to spill out of.
These rocks I found need a job to do.

I started this earlier
But my strength is gone
And my breath leaves suddenly
Like a shy and anxious visitor.

And maybe you will enjoy it too,
These flowers on fire
And sage leaves spilling
As you come and go.

So I set to work
(or a more serious form of play)
Putting one rock on another
Nestling them into the slope and each other.
And she sat on her stoop companionably,
Speaking of nothing at all.

Within an hour it was done
And there among the rocks and flowers
We both left some small part of ourselves
In that small wall.

GERARD DONNELLY SMITH

The Real Estate Sale

Under the carport, box after box
of books spill out: some well-read
others like new, spines unbroken:
the *Norton Anthology of English Lit.*
a Shakespeare glossary,
a copy of *As You Like It*,
the collected work
of Tennessee Williams
among the discarded,
headed to a thrift store,
and more glassware than
one person could ever need:
tumblers, pints, champagne flutes
and in each set one or two broken, and
"I love you, mom",
and happy anniversary mugs,
all for free; the unshattered sets,
priced at a few dollars, are sparkly clean.
An upright piano, dusty,
and possibly, slightly out of tune;
no sheet music anywhere.
There are, of course, nick-knacks,
quilts, jewelry, and mementos
that she may carry with her,
but that no one else will know.
And the house itself, a shamble,
and then up the stairs,
in the bedrooms,
the plaster crumbling,
the lathe turning to dust,
the asbestos ceiling tiles
painted white and sagging
from God knows what, suddenly.
an overwhelming melancholy
and claustrophobia drives

me downstairs and outside, holding
the Stevie Ray Vaughan CDs
I bought from her survivors.

When I listen to them, I will
remember this person
that I never knew.

NORA SNYDER

A Christmas Plan That Became a Christmas Unplanned… and Led by the Itching of my Fingertips

All the little components started shedding like pine needles.
An early work drop off, a leaving while I slept, a sad cancellation that felt bigger like
A giant pregnant tear full of past losses

Hold commitments with an open palm.
Remain appreciative and unattached.
Don't let them bite your fingers.

Resurrection,
the scent of salmon and hot rice,
The call of cheese from my people (two, just in case)
And the surprise—an essential slice of the holiday

Gifts on our backs, food in our arms, gone visiting
Our son just cracking awake from the night shift
His little apartment dim but cozy
All my heart wanted was to see his long body
Draped along the sectional

LIANE SOUSA
Silence

No television or radio blaring,
no cat meowing or dog whining.
Just me sitting on the patio
enjoying this bright spring day,
noticing the flowers budding
and plants sprouting while
a white butterfly flutters about.

Slowly, I am aware of a
lizard sunning on the bricks,
hummingbirds feeding,
seagulls circling in the sky,
and bees pollinating.

I hear scurrying in the leaves,
chirping at the feeder,
squawking above,
and buzzing at nearby blooms.

An abundance of Nature's symphony—
better than silence.

KIM STAFFORD
Bagel Boy

I don't know how I got the notion,
the year before I was a man, when
poor but rich in time and whimsy—
to raise a dough heap on a dusty board,
tear off fists to roll and coil in rings
dropped in my boiling cauldron until
they glistened, then briefly baked to be
looped by a cord slung over my shoulder
so I could ride my bike through town
offering friends and strangers a warm gift
my hands had made. What have I done since
with half the wisdom of that foolishness?

KRISTINA STAPLETON
Escape of the MS Rotterdam

Boat with the night to itself
cruises the shipping lane
in full regalia of light
while her passengers sleep.

I watch with my coffee
from the sidelines with trees
between us, twizzling the light
into a dazzle of sparks.

This is the last ship of the season
leaving the harbor in October to crawl
between continents through the canal
and emerge newborn into the tropics.

I stay behind with the spiders,
the canned cider and the order
of a cord of stacked wood, to rock
away under a burden of cold to come.

JOHN STICKNEY
Future Visit

All my misplaced commas
Have found a new home
In the Bad Punctuation Museum

I owe them a visit

D. YOHANNA STORM

My High Priestess of Prayer

She would laugh if she knew I called her this:
The High Priestess of Prayer
We are unlikely friends
I'm a devout unbeliever in dogma, though
I once gave the dominant paradigm
my rapt attention

I evolved agnosticated,
a devout gardener, spontaneously musical,
at times, making my own
joyful noise
unto the Spirits

I'm a poet, reverent/irreverent,
kind, tender, pacifist, progressive,
loyal friend, shelterer,
lyricist

Spiritually available, I light
the candles and balefires
on all the high holy days

I have found sacred grace in
the earth beneath my feet
Student of life, no longer a seeker
She… is Christian, joyously born again
having been wrung about by life,
Found the elusive thing she can take shelter in

No ordinary, vanilla Christian,
Lizzy with her spiky hair, infectious laugh,
her honest kitchen always filled
with grandchildren, and
the language of fresh cookies
Life couldn't wring the juice from her!

But she was good with prayer
It was her thing, not mine so much

I feel strange anytime I call her, in a pinch
to ask if she would pray for
someone I care about or
sometimes—me

It's like borrowing a cup of sugar
and after the seventh or eighth time, why
haven't I bought my own damned sugar?

I don't pray because I failed at prayer
I'm a distorted cartoon of that pious Catholic kid
in the front pew, a wannabe disciple
at sunrise Mass before school,
tagging along with my dad

There's no padded kneeler in the
front pew, so I knelt
on that cold marble floor
with my naked, third-grade knees
like some small shriven apostle
while my dad read from the book and
prayed
as the priest prepared the offering

I poured so much of my youthful
holy water—tears into fervent beseeching:

Please, God answer me
Help my mom feel better
Let her next baby come out safe
Help me pass my math test
Please make the war stop and our
beloved President, JFK
come back to life
But most of all, God
Help me believe

I prayed
Figured I'd be heard someday
among the humans bleeding from the war
or above the love-rock music,
above the sonic booms of aircraft, breaking
the sound barrier above our family garden

Distracted,
I prayed

I even toyed with the idea of becoming a nun,
so maybe the mystery would be revealed

I prayed
I failed

Life and heartache intervene,
Tears and not one of my fervent entreaties answered

I suspect I should be grateful that some things
didn't happen that could have

But Lizzy, with her bright pink hair and
her even brighter faith,
her many grandchildren, is but a
phone call away

The High Priestess prays,
Things happen.

Another cup of sugar.

MARK STROHSCHEIN

Let Me Begin Again

after Major Jackson

Let me begin again as a heron
caught up in a long game of contemplation
stretching thin legs in mud. Waiting. Being.
Divining that home is a beautifully bitter place.
Let me begin as an anvil that can take
the hot hammering—like the *Ānebolt* of my
German ancestors who fire-forged.
The way their thin blood boiled under
coldness & adherence to precision. Except
let me begin again by showing more
than the raw strength of the strike. Let me
learn to hum to the heart's music.
Let me never be the dry blue blood
of resignation, the purple bruise
of never having loved enough, the welt
of weakness—of lacking strength
to journey to that singular Island of Me,
subsumed by waves from a calm sea.
Reader, before it's too late & your
magic mirror loses the power it possesses,
begin again as the cloud that pours
every inch of its rain-soul back into the
solemn earth. Let me, in the lateness
of the hour, begin again. Softly. Wings
at rest in the unflappable marshland of my mind.

JESSICA SWAFFORD
To Tell the Cats

The hardest part was to tell the cats
you wouldn't return home—EVER.
That was worse than telling people.

I told them we'd always celebrate
'treat thirty' in your honor.
They suddenly weren't as hungry.

Chopper stopped spinning in circles.
Playing string wasn't as fun
without your encouragements and wrist flips.

They were scared before the ambulance
carried you away—too many people.
More first responders than I could count.

None off you like(d) crowds or even people really.
They hid wondering why I'd allow it
as if I had control over anything.

DAVID M. SWEET

Turning a Corner

It began with dusk sleepy on hillsides:
the first spring peepers called to each other
with a willingness to put behind
the previous week's snow
and a pond lately skimmed with thinning ice.

Maybe it was that warmer than usual breeze
the very first of February
when old daffodils reared tired, tiny heads
through soft loam and leaves
to see if a new sun would pay a visit.

The time appeared right when morning cardinals
in barren dogwoods burned just bright enough
to throw me some hope:
a corner waited just ahead of me
If I chose to peer into the unknown.

As I gazed into cobalt skies above,
I knew: I'm alive.
Alive, like those years (young and innocent)
counting robins for Mama in March or
climbing apple trees blooming in April.

I'd turned a corner to shorter streets, less
ahead than behind, but those I embrace
with light on my face: a soul more balanced
between past/present,
between good/evil,
between myself/I.

Oh yeah, Life goes on
long after the dread
of living goes on—
I walk on.

CONNIE TAYLOR
A Duck's Back

Let the churning waters of life
roll off my mind and heart
as though from a duck's back.

Free experience from fear,
familiarity from distrust,
perspective from apprehension.

Spread my wings into the skies
of the new year with joy,
playfulness, exuberance, thankfulness.

JO TAYLOR
Tacos, Cracks and Song

Today I walk the shadowed path at noon
to the town square, careful my flipflops
don't hang on the raised and broken stones
of Lyda Sue Lane, up the hill and to the right,
through dogwoods decked out for spring.
I trudge past First Baptist Church and
the Lucky Day Taco and Tequila Bar, stopping
at the window of the vinyls and skateboards shop
to study the skeleton's mocking and twisted torso
like that of the Mona Lisa in the Louvre. *What
will you do with these brief hours and days? What
will you offer the path?* Suddenly, the day brightens,
and the blood-stained flowers raise their heads, and
the cracks in the sidewalk transform into art. I, too,
lift my head towards the heavens and offer a prayer
of thanksgiving. For seventy-one seasons
of the dogwood in bloom. For tacos and shadows
and sunshine and song. For asphalt fissures and
concrete cracks. For the thistles that push up
through them.

DAWN THOMPSON
Thaw

I am listening for thaw
even though this morning the air
is as cold as hunger.
Still, the buttery sun hangs in the sky,
an ancient oracle of good fortune.
Still, the light comes earlier every day as
flocks of geese travel in a confident arrow
to shores of green shoots, ice returning to water.

Where I have frozen, become stuck, hardened,
I am beginning to hear the drip, drip
of melting, of surrender.
I am beginning to see the push, push
of old seeds I'd forgotten I'd planted.
And there, when I close my eyes,
I am beginning to feel the hum, hum
of some final shedding
as the new season of light opens and sings.

Why not let the light in?
Who am I to lock the windows
when just outside a band is playing?

DAVID TRAYLOR
New Flyer

#3 Jackson
       Sullen sitting shadows
#206 Evanston Circulator
       Waiting in the rain
#82 Kimball / Homan
       Shrouded by hoods and darkness
#30 Stockton
       A curiosity for passing cars
#24 Wentworth
       Frozen in the headlights
#54 Felton
       Pay driver upon entry
#52 Excelsior
       Exact fare only

#28 19th Street
       Moving forward
#1 Bronzeville / Union Station
       Symphony of road noise
#218 Evanston Connector
       Rhythms and rests
#78 Montrose
       A driver like a conductor
#156 Northgate
       Tapping each beat, each stop
#43 Masonic
       Every day except for Sundays and Holidays
#54 Felton
       Express only

#126 Jackson
       A salon on wheels
#88 Higgins
       Family for a moment
#92 Foster
       New arrivals, late departures

#35 Eureka
    No surprises here
#31 Balboa
    On and off
#136 LaSalle Express
    Same old story
#151 Sheridan
    Stand behind the line
#106 Aurora
    Need a transfer
#155 Melrose
    Next stop

#38 Geary
    Sorry out of service
#99 San Bruno Night Owl
    End of the line

KATHRYN TRUE
The Balance of Things

Red crossbills scrape their songs from willing branches,
  as an orb weaver plucks meaning into her endless mandala.
On the creek, water striders glide in the superaquatic.
Living on the threshold, they are unperturbed by the in-between.
Caddisfly larvae wrapped in leaves traverse the creek bottom,
  lining up on a muddy runway to the stars.
An orange-bright butterfly passes by as a cipher,
  encoding the daydreams of a red-legged frog.
Perhaps just as horses synchronize their heartbeats,
  the trees align their internal pulses with our own—
  guiding our continual reckoning with rupture and peace.
Breathe in, breathe out.
No, really—breathe.
A V of geese keeps the balance of things.

GAIL HATHAWAY TUPPER
Untitled

There are two ways to go about it.
One, which I have already practiced,
is to speculate at great length
and hesitate,
cross out and crumple,
consider every outset
and every destination
before taking a step.

The other, unfolding now, is to
take a step.
Yes, it's slippery
but you know the terrain
and you will be ok.
This is the way,
you knew it all along:
early morning,
the dog and the cup
and the open book.
Welcome.

LESLEY TYSON
The Dream Was a Lie

lost in a dream maze that i pretend
i don't recognize as familiar
because i didn't want it to be
anything close to real that
would explain the salt crust
trailing down from my eye

fleeting glimpses of pillar lined nave
i can breathe the residue of sadness
seeping out between the pillars
each decorated with their own abstractions
of the altars they contain and the doors
waiting to be opened

i wanted to rest in the between but
each altar insisted on revealing its history
and i always curious to let myself
be caught in their unique chaos where
i could not save or be saved only able
to watching burning the flooding

weeping in the surrealistic aftermath
of legends i never understood so tears
slid down my cheeks as i seemed to run
back the empty nave only to find him
waiting for me as i dreamed so often
but it was lie as always just another way

he still taunts me from some past
where we were not the actors and
i had not forgotten my lines again and
he had not tried to put words in my mouth
except this night i was so bereft
from witnessing broken worlds i cursed him
to silence as i walk to the exit

MARY VEE
Ice

Ice retreats from water.
Though armed with snowy cover
He faces Lake's glassy stare.

Ice remains poised and dares
Lake to embrace him.
She ripples. Sweeps forward, and brims.
… Kissing him.

Ice, knowing her warm touch
Will melt his heart—
Chooses, on this wintry day, not to part.

But remains at her shore.
Till temperatures drop once more…
And she has need of him.

JAYNE R. VONDRAK
In the Honeycomb of My Bones

Each syllable's flavor
is tangy on tongue,
warms my throat,
as I drink words from ancient
pages, from grandmother's
stories, from holy air.

Language gathers, fills hollows,
nourishes every cell.
Sweetness ferments
in the honeycomb of my bones
until every bit of marrow swells,
every vessel bursts into syrup.
Heart pulses mystical meanings,
sense permeates each organ.
Breath circulates measured
lines until syntax
seeps through soles,
leaves tracks for others
to consume or follow.

LYNN J. WALTERS

Blessings and Love

The blessings of the Mother
        be upon you.
She who is the pink of dawn,
        the blanket of stars at night,
        the trees and deep roots,
        past all the layers of humanity.
Flowers dormant, in bloom, and extinct.
Playful as a squirrel,
        protective as a bear.
Yet encompassing immeasureable love
        for all creation.
Even—especially—you.

CATHY WARNER
Morning Prayer

In memory of William Stafford and in gratitude to Kim Stafford

I prepare the order of worship
for Sunday's Morning Prayer with Eucharist
a service we begin on our knees
praying before The Father asking
for "those things necessary
for our life and salvation."

Though it is only Wednesday
at the poetry reading
I am offered the prayers
of The Father by his Son.
Morning's first thoughts
scrawled on blank pages.
The Son's own words—
his eternal desire for peace—
a mirror of his Father's.

The Holy Spirit hovers over
The Father and The Son,
ritual of pen and flame
revelation and creation.
At the altar I kneel, hands
cupped as they pour forth
those things so necessary
for our life and salvation.

SETH WARREN
Island of the Narrow

Island of the narrow
Sleep upon no shoulders

Dunes become us
Sandblown and riverside

Flowing from a borealis
Hysterical
Where no drones are allowed

Follow arctic cod to hot pots
Serving alcohol in saga water
Preserving timberlines in dreams

Burst through novice tourist bubbles
Crossing over time
Even dying
Risking mud
Fueling the survival furnace
We all must stoke

CRYSTAL L. WHITE
What Dream Touches

What dream touches
the ritual of sleep? A black

hole appears in broad
light. Matter so bleak its
force magnificently
disarms the strongest of wills. You:

wired-electric, anxiously carving
spaces between air—
unnerving ice cracks the side

walks off slightly—
stutter-step on rooftop edges
Blankets just out of reach, we

glimpse Time:
flowing again. A fleeting star
cluster found at our fingertips, a
place for everything. The first
rest in years.

JENNIFER R. WHITE
The Gift of Ages

The fruits of time
May set us free
Even as lines colonize our faces
As hair greys and skin thins
We've learned our lessons
Put in our hours
Paid the mage price over and over again
suffering and hard learning
Then joy!
We graduate from this school of life
reaping the fruits of our soul's journey—
change and growth
self-knowledge and wisdom
Our contract with time fulfilled
Now we can be whole at last
Reborn in the afternoon of life
Living with holy joy

BRENDA WILDRICK

Flames Rapidly Spreading

After *When Death Comes* by Mary Oliver

Referencing news from March 1, 2024, including the death of Alexei Navalny, a fearless Russian political opposition leader who died in prison after years of torture

In Moscow, cold stones of the Quench My Sorrows
Church can't feel our distant tears. The crowd
gathered for an illegal funeral chants—
Putin is a murderer!—
Silence is not an option, even in this time
of unprecedented repression, even in this time
when the USA *snaps the purse shut*
against aid for Ukraine.

In Texas, fire consumes the panhandle,
while on the southern border, caustic politics toss
in gasoline and lit matches, and first responders
struggle to cope with the mental strain of their daily
recovery of decomposing bodies.
This is a whole different monster—they say.

In Gaza, aid for the starving is airdropped,
as it becomes increasingly dangerous to bring
trucks into the fire of gunshots and bombs. And death
like a *hungry bea*r devours hundreds more each day.

Mary Oliver, I, too, want to be *a bride married
to amazement, the bridegroom taking the world
in my arms.* But the world is burning. It is much
too hot to touch.

Still, like cleansing water flowing, like hope splashing,
I offer this prayer:
may we cease to be *frightened* and *full of argument*,
may we, together, build spaces where solutions

are dreamed and created,
may airdropped tears refresh heroes and multiply
their courage into miracles,
may miracles quench the flames of sorrow
and cool our burning world.

DANA WILDSMITH

Everything Else Falls Away

> *"For me, writing is physical joy. It is almost sexual—not the moment of fulfillment, but the moment when you open the door to where your lover is waiting and everything else falls away."*   —Lee Smith

The blank page is the door.
The words you possess are a ring of keys.
You try one after the other
until a word fits
and notions tumble into language.
Everything else falls away,
including the door.

TIM WILES
Safe at Home

I have chosen not to go
To the baseball game
40 miles away
Which will be played
This evening
In a wooden grandstand ballpark, built in 1892
101 years after
Some ancient baseball rules
Were found in that town.

Only three games will be played there
This year. There will be two more chances.
That's how baseball is.

I love the game,
But would rather
Sit here on this porch with our dog
Waiting for my wife and son
To come home.

JAKE WILLIAMS
To an Easter Craiglockhart Elm

My leaves whisper of your histories
as your drums salute your stones
Leith waters ask for their rain and your surprise
so, we watch your revolutions pass and red stars decay
flags fall with our leaves

While sap flows through my young veins
clouds pass, butterfly chases butterfly
my seeds carry life on the winds
your wounds cannot be healed
by your hands alone

Steel storms arise
pictures pass in peaty waters
where are the Doves now?
My leaves still whisper to your young wonder

STEVE WILLIAMS
Proper Space and Shape?

Gaza's ungraved bodies,
Ukraine's broken shrines

The sunset that is coming,
        the dawn we left behind

The place best left there empty,

      the word with luck we find

Is there enough space,
of the right kind,
to give your poem
the shape
it needs,
deserves?

JESSICA WOLF
I Know Love

Your lips brush my shoulder
As you pull me closer
In the cool darkness of your room

Our awareness settles then
But you reel me back in—
"What's your middle name again?"

Your words, barely coherent—
Like this question burned you
Blazing straight through
The drowsy in-between

Needing to know me—
More, and better
Right now, even here
In our twilight serenity

I smile into the darkness
Press myself closer into you
In that moment, I know love

Your arms around me so warm
Your love for me a slow burn
In the cool darkness of your room

BETH WOLFE
I'm Not Here to Smile Because it Makes You Happy

The mask of a smile
that doesn't reach the eyes
deceives the foolish
and self-absorbed,
those distracted by their own cares.

It's the mask we keep at hand,
ready to display in a split second
when the truth weighs too much
to lift and push forward.

It's the mask demanded
by those who can't accept
their complicity in the wariness
we bear.

Smile, they say
and we oblige, in part,
but curses flow from behind
our clinched teeth.

GLORIA WU
Inextinguishable

There once was a boy,
In a bookstore he worked.
He was sweet and kind,
His boss wanted him to be a mime.

Mime he was not,
For this boy's voice was mighty as a sword.
He brightened the days of those who walked in,
Especially mine.
His voice carried warmth and love,
In both greetings and goodbyes.

Lots of things at this store he learned,
That you catch more flies with honey than fight.
When the intoxicated wanted entry,
As happened many a night,
This boy used his voice
In ways no others had done,
With his very own brand of ahimsa
And a touch of his light.

The very boss who wanted him to be a mime
Did not possess the ability to make his dream real.
Did not know how, himself, to be kind.
Did not understand the virtue of respect.
And so, the boy and he fought.
Not out of hatred,
But because they held different values.
The boy cared about respect, and his boss did not.

As the days went on, the boy got by.
The light within him still burned,
Though day by day, a little less bright.
Until one day,
The boy delivered some unfortunate news.
Like a fuse gone mad,
The boss grabbed him with a jarring boom.

And it was then,
The fire that had been slowly dying
LIT ABLAZE—
Brighter than any star,
Louder than any lion,
More aware than any feline.

Don't you dare touch me!
The boy lit—
Livid and alive.
Flames he could no longer hold back,
Flames he would no longer dim,
Flames that once fueled his soul, rebirthed
That starry, violent night.

He stood tall.
A man, instead of a boy.
His sword wielded,
Not to slice,
But only to defend.

The man walked out of the prison disguised as books.
When he did, the world stood still—
Eyes wide, hearts open,
Hands lifted in cheer.
A sigh and a smile
Broke free from his lips.
For light in him and those around him was restored,
Blazing once more,

Inextinguishable.

DIOSA XOCHIQUETZACLCÓATL
At a Library Somewhere in SoCal

I couldn't help but notice,
the way he threw his car door into my parked vehicle,
not bothering to apologize,
though all four windows were down in my car
as I sat in the front seat.

I couldn't help but notice
how I sat in my front seat and watched this *wasichu*
glance at me through my side view mirror,
then walk away like nothing had happened.

I couldn't help but notice
how the one Mexican-American poet
who took the time to name-drop
was enthusiastically invited to submit bilingual poems
though she never spoke a single word of Spanish.

I couldn't help but notice
how reading poetry in my mother tongue
still tends to surprise people,
especially people from the borderlands,
from a city that carries a name
in the same language as my poems.

I couldn't help but notice
on the long, lonely drive back home
how I was proudly wearing my *huipíl* and my *huaraches*
and how society still tends to judge a book by its cover.

ANYA ZAMIAR
Street Crossing

for Danielle

After my friend
was run over by that dump truck
and bled out in the street,
a block from her home,
calling her husband's name:
I don't cross the street the same.

I used to look to the horizon, or to my feet,
exactly where I was headed—
confident and poised—
something too lovely
to possibly destroy.
However, now I look
each fucker in the eye,
as if to say, "Look upon me!"
"I fucking dare you;
fuck with me!"
Still poised and confident,
now ready for a fight—
more menacing in the eyes.
Because I'll be damned
if that's how I'm going
to meet my demise.

It won't be in the fucking street
when I die.

NORMA ZIMMERMANN

Ship Wrecked

Cars from the distant highway
sound like the surf,
waves crashing at 65 mph.

Mile markers go by like buoys,
bobbing on the side of the road,
while exit sign lifeguards look on.

Salty gasoline air,
diesel, regular, premium,
drift over the tops of the trees,
and reach me on my deck,

reminding me of sitting in my canvas beach chair,
burning in the sweaty July heat,
burying my toes in the coarse Atlantic sand.

A cop car goes by, flashing blue,
an ambulance streaking red.
Someone is in trouble,
drowning in the cloverleaf
riptide.

Poetry Unlocked My Jail Cell: Our Stafford Challenge Parting Poem

A collaborative poem written by the 2024 cohort of
The Stafford Challenge

The river, passing, yes, is never gone
Curiosity pulsing till the final breath
Though I step away, the voices continue

From waiting to losing to heaven...
My bare feet steeped in frost, rooted in the dark—
The end has only just begun.

Discord, lost, remembering I'm connected
7,300 poems left to go; a lifetime begun
I turn the page and begin again

Forward with strangers turned into friends
I stood, inhaled, and stepped forth
Here we sit, tethered by our words

To join with other voices
Tender green buds became fiery blossoms
Does the seed die when it opens?

From waiting to losing to heaven...
What may come along the path
A prisoner once

Everything so prone to breakage
I'm eating my tail again
Endings and beginnings become one

It was dark at the beginning
Lie in the grass, keep dreaming
Before I ever began, the end had me beguiled

Until we are parted by death
A basket-full of poems delivered at the doorstep
I dreamt of falling. I never landed

Finally, zipped into the flannel-lined sleeping bag, the stars fell
Pain poured through my pen
Wild butterflies linger still, asleep

It changed me because I let it.

Beginning not seeking a finish but a journey—
First words or last lines; keep writing.

Poetry unlocked my cell
Discord, lost, remembering I'm connected
Beginning not seeking a finish but a journey

The best endings are also beginnings
I stitched stories together because you also were sowing
Not a beginning or an ending, continuing

I near, never touching, journey's end
Write the poem and set it free
2024 will be reborn as a book

It's finished. Now, we can begin.
A prisoner once, poetry unlocked my cell
Heart quickens with life

Beats ecstatic, pause, beat, complete
Connect and reconnect, that's what writing is all about
Staring into the dark until the light appears

A thousand seeds each sprouting its own wispy parachute
Small, timid, a blank page fills
Suspended in this silent symphony, I listen

Being roped in, it's time to let go and fly
In my goodbye, remembering our hello
Pouring thoughts on page as therapy

Seeds of thoughts… bouquet of friends
I draw the curtains and step away
Open the window, the world rushes in

A year of words to paper
Roots transform to wings and fly
Cuddled the wee hours away

It changed me because I let it.

You made all the difference
Sifting thoughts lead to mosaic understanding.

Wheeling through time space beginnings endings merge
Something forgotten remembered again
Enlightened and enriched we grow

William Stafford's practice of writing a poem (or scrap of a poem) every morning became the inspiration for the creation of The Stafford Challenge.

ABOUT WILLIAM STAFFORD

William Stafford (1914-1993) was one of the most prolific and important American poets of the last half of the twentieth century.

He was born in Hutchinson, Kansas, served as a conscientious objector in a series of work camps during World War II, and taught for 30 years at Lewis & Clark College in Oregon, as well as traveling the world to share the gospel of poetry.

Among his many credentials, Stafford served as consultant in poetry at the Library of Congress (the name was later changed to the US Poet Laureate), and received the National Book Award for his poetry collection *Traveling through the Dark* (1963). He also served as Oregon Poet Laureate from 1975 to 1990. During his lifetime, Stafford published over 60 books of poetry that still resonate with both scholars and general readers, and a dozen books by and about him have been published since his death.

He was famous for his habit of daily writing, for his "be not afraid to fail" verve as a writer, and for his kindness and welcome as a teacher. "Let's talk recklessly," he would say, and the conversation, the class, the poem would lift from there.

www.ingramcontent.com/pod-product-compliance
Lightning Source LLC
Chambersburg PA
CBHW020353170426

43200CB00005B/151